COMMON THREADS
ten life stories

michele Candleand

COMMON THREADS
ten life stories

How Women Weave
Tribulation into Triumph

MICHELLE CANDLAND

Life Tapestry Press • Alpine, California

Candland, Michelle.

Common threads : ten life stories: how women weave tribulation into triumph / Michelle Candland. -- Alpine, CA : Life Tapestry Press, c2010.

   p. ; cm.

   ISBN: 978-0-9770796-0-5
   Includes index.

1. Women--Psychology. 2. Life change events--Psychological aspects--Case studies. 3. Self-esteem in women. 4. Self-actualization (Psychology) 5.Women--Conduct of life. 6. Achievement motivation in women. I. Title.

HQ2037 .C36 2010
646.7/0082--dc22   1004

PUBLISHER: Life Tapestry Press
           3930 Via Palo Verde Lago
           Alpine, CA 91901
           (619) 517-4453

A BookStudio Production, *www.bookstudiobooks.com*
Produced by Karla Olson
Copyedited by Lisa Wolff
Cover and interior design by TLC Graphics, *www.TLCGraphics.com*

www. michellecandland.com

Dedication

This book is dedicated to my husband, Art, who has never stopped living our marriage vows to celebrate one another's existence, and to my sons, Troy and Justin, who have always been the light at the end of my tunnel.

Acknowledgments

Common Threads is a compilation of almost 60 years of my personal experiences, ranging from early childhood memories, to adult "ah ha!" moments. It is a collection of little somethings that would later prove to be the cause of big somethings, joyful muses, sad observations, sources of pride, causes of embarrassment, and even periods of disgrace. All are threads of experience that are woven together to make up my life tapestry. There were times when I thought I had more unraveling than weaving going on; times when the texture was loose, the colors were dark, and the pattern was ill conceived. Other times, the edges of the images were precise, the colors were rich, and the big picture was filled with both accomplishment and hope for a brighter tomorrow.

The chapters in this book are complemented with the stories of other women who have been an inspiration to me and who have taken their own artistic license to weave something special when they could have settled for the status quo.

The courageous women described in these chapters have either told their stories to me personally or have been documented by acknowledged sources. I share their journeys along with mine with the hope that our experiences will encourage others to explore and expand their own individual horizons.

My personal dream to complete this book would have remained just a dream if I hadn't been introduced to Karla Olson, the founder of BookStudio. Her multi-dimensional understanding of the entire book industry along with her authentic guidance and sincere desire to help me succeed was truly a gift. I can only give my thanks and my allegiance to work with her on my books in the years to come.

But I didn't just bump into Karla in the grocery store. Our clandestine meeting was a product of taking a risk—sharing my dream with one person who led me to another who led me to Karla. And Karla led me to MonkeyC-Media, TLC Graphics, Ollie Media, United Graphics, all of whom played a vital role in the realization of this project.

My family and friends have been an amazing support system. My best friend and husband, Art, was instrumental in pushing me to take my dog-eared draft to the next level and has complete confidence I will enjoy great success. Unconditional love is a wonderful thing! All six of the children in our blended marriage have been a source of bubbly encouragement, and I am so blessed to be a part of their lives.

I spent countless hours sitting beside my mother's bed during her final weeks of life, and when she slept, I wrote. Although she didn't live long enough to see the final product, I'm hopeful she would be proud of my efforts. I will

ACKNOWLEDGEMENTS

always be grateful for her example of courage and continuous nudge to keep me moving forward.

Common Threads wasn't written in a vacuum. It has been infused with my environment and enriched by all those around me. Thank you to all those who never stopped believing in me and for giving me the courage to believe in myself.

Table of Contents

Introduction

A Psychic Prediction

Over the years, my personal belief system has been shaped by countless people, ideas, thoughts, and experiences. I've always believed that there is a power greater than myself, that the universal mind will carry thoughts at warp speed to anyone who is open to receiving them, that the power of positive thought will produce tangible results, and that we are the masters of our own destiny. I also believe we are all here to accomplish something special. That said, I also know from personal experience that nothing worthwhile comes easily.

When I was about 19 years old I was talking to some coworkers about people who claim to possess psychic powers. One young woman mentioned she had recently visited a psychic and offered to provide his contact information. Who wouldn't want to know what her future had to offer? I called the number on the business card and made an appointment to see him the following Saturday.

The small office was located in a two-story building in desperate need of maintenance. The gray-blue stucco that had not peeled off from repeated water damage was faded, the wood around the door was cracking, and what had once been a flowerbed was now just a muddy patch of dirt butted against a dry strip of dead grass. When I entered the dimly lit room, my eyes were immediately drawn to a heavy-set, middle-aged man with thinning hair and a dark goatee seated behind a large dark brown desk. The edges of the desk and the shelves behind were covered with dozens of small blue Smurf dolls. *What's wrong with this picture?* I asked myself.

Apparently my puzzled look was pretty obvious. When my gaze went from the Smurfs back to the man behind the desk, he was smiling. "I've been collecting them for years," he said.

We made our formal introductions, and then he preceded our official business with this observation: "I'm not going to tell you anything you don't already know. I'm just going to bring it to the forefront of your mind. What I see may not come to pass in the near future and it may not happen for years." He then asked whether I wanted to begin with any specific questions.

I did, of course. Would I have any children? Would they live long lives? Would I be successful in my job? Would I ever make a difference in anyone's life but my own? His answers were, "Yes, you will have two sons and you will enjoy a very special relationship with one of your grandsons. You will be successful beyond your expectations, and you will touch the lives of hundreds or even thousands of children you will never even meet." Wow, really? He also said he could read my aura and asked whether I was dealing with stress in my life. At the time I was plagued with all sorts of issues in my romantic relationship, my family, and my job. I wondered how he could tell, and he said that my aura was yellow and orange and radiated at least a foot from my body. My aura? This required a fuller explanation and with only a few minutes remaining in my one-hour session, he inquired about a return visit. I scheduled another appointment in a month.

On my drive home, I thought about the psychic's observations. *How could all this information have been something I already knew?*

The next time I visited the Smurf psychic, he said I must have been busy because my aura was a cool green and blue and extended a few inches from my skin. Come to think of it, I was feeling much more contented.

The psychic began to explain that despite my calmer aura, he was seeing opposing visions. I would have two sons who would live long lives, but they would each have a close brush with death at an early age. I would earn seven figures, but I would experience financial ruin. I would be deeply loved, but I would be physically and emotionally abused. How could all this be true? It would all hinge on personal choices and their consequences.

The following pages are not filled with intellectual theories or cerebral observations. Instead, they are a compilation of life lessons, reminders, and real experiences of women from all walks of life. They are treasures that come from my mistakes and triumphs, as well as the missteps and rewards of women across the country and around the globe. They are the common threads of wisdom that unite us in the universal journey through tribulation to triumph, over and over again.

I like to imagine each of us is weaving her own life tapestry. Each thread is symbolic of an experience, an emotion, a joy, a loss, a success, or a failure. Some are rough and nubby, some are smooth as silk, some are the color of dark, painful shadows and others are crimson red and sunset orange; they all combine to create our own unique pattern.

In these pages, I won't be telling you anything you don't already know. I'll just be confirming your innermost feelings; you are unique, you are capable, you are not alone, and you are worth it.

When you've completed this journey it is my hope that you will have a renewed sense of direction, be armed with some tools to assist you in your next adventure, and feel strengthened by the knowledge that you are surrounded by others who truly wish you great success in everything you do. You will be more prepared to weave with clear intention.

chapter one

Because You're Worth It

*The willingness to accept responsibility for one's own life
is the source from which self-respect springs.*

JOAN DIDION

Children learn at a very young age that there is one skill that is more important than all the rest, and that acquiring this skill makes the years ahead manageable. That skill is learning to negotiate. Even as a young child you negotiated: for treats, privileges, and arguments; about chores, dates, and job offers.

There is one thing, however, that is never, ever negotiable, and that is your right to self-respect. Having self-respect is the one specific principle that will make your life less complicated and more content.

— COMMON THREAD —

You learn what you live.

Unfortunately, not every child is brought up to believe that he or she is a gift, a worthwhile individual who possesses the potential to help change the world, one person at a time. If your parents weren't taught self-respect as children, then it is likely they did not give you that valuable nugget either.

But that doesn't mean you can't *learn* to respect yourself. It's never too late to discover more about yourself, your strengths and weaknesses, and how you can use your attributes to become what you define as a valuable, participating, self-respecting individual.

Personal Accounting

It is a good idea, every six months or so, to take a personal inventory of yourself. Sit in a quiet place, ask yourself these questions, and be brutally honest with your answers. You will be surprised at what you will learn about yourself.

- What makes you proud?
- What brings you joy?
- What makes you smile?
- Are you the best you can be, or is there room for improvement?
- Are you honest with yourself?
- Are you authentic around others?
- Can you help others learn the value of self-respect?

Think carefully about your answers. Do you like what you see? If not, what steps can you take to make a change for the better?

— COMMON THREAD —

Respect and love yourself so you can help others to do the same.

Scott Blanchard, a well-known writer and public speaker, describes the concept of making changes that are congruent with what he calls self-love as "radical self-acceptance." It's what I call self-respect. He writes that radical self-acceptance occurs when "we are in a position to leverage our strengths to the point where our weaknesses are irrel-evant." It is self-encouragement rather than predetermined failure. It is unconditional acceptance and celebration of who you are, with your unique value and special abilities. Once you've reached this internal place of quiet strength, you can lead others to places they never dreamed they could go.

This Zen-like mindset was not instilled in me as a child. I cultivated it only after 40 years of self-doubt and unsuccessful relationships.

The oldest of four and the only girl, I was raised to be a responsible Pleaser—someone who strives to make everyone around him or her comfortable and happy, who goes out of the way to avoid negative feedback or conflict. I watched my mother try to perfect the art of pleasing as a survival mechanism, and I struggled to emulate her. The problem was that I witnessed her failures along with her successes, and I didn't understand how to separate the two. Therefore, my limited experience with relationships included the subconscious acceptance of blame and abuse.

I often felt responsibility for the feelings and actions of others, when they really had nothing to do with me and were not in my control. Instead of trusting what my gut told me, I tried to fix the situation so it wasn't uncom-fortable anymore—just as my mother did. It took me a long time to snip the thread she had handed me and tie on a new fiber of my own.

— COMMON THREAD —

If something feels wrong, it usually is.

When I was only four or five, I had already been so conditioned to please and avoid conflict that I didn't protest when my best friend's father molested me. We were playing hide-and-seek; my friend was counting and her dad and I were looking for a place to hide. He suggested we climb into a large cabinet in the garage and I hurriedly joined him. The space was small, so I had to sit in front of him between his legs. He wrapped his arms around me and whispered that he had a present for me. He said he would put the shiny marble in my pocket but when he "missed" and it went into my pants, he went after it. When I resisted his purposeful fondling, he told me to be quiet. I was terrified but afraid to say anything. I tried to wriggle away and he finally retrieved the marble. He said this would be a secret and we shouldn't tell my dad because it would make him very angry. He even offered me a shiny quarter to keep our secret. I've never told anyone about that experience. Until now...

Writing this book has given me perspective on my life, and I believe my lessons are universal. Pay attention to your own threads and textures, as they add richness to your life tapestry.

— COMMON THREAD —

Every childhood experience prepares you for life, one way or another.

I spent my teen years going to school, working in the family dry-cleaning shop, and taking care of my three brothers. I was living proof that the rules are usually more strict for the firstborn and for girls. I wasn't allowed to have friends over or spend the night with other girls, and I wasn't allowed to wear makeup or go on a date until I was 16. That, of course, didn't stop me from trying to be like my peer group. I tried to have a boyfriend and go to parties and do the things that popular girls were doing. Those efforts required breaking the rules set by my parents, sneaking out to meet my boyfriend, and eventually paying the price.

I was a freshman in high school and utterly smitten with a senior. One afternoon when my parents were working, I sneaked out of the house and went for a ride with my first real boyfriend in his very cool midnight-blue 1957 Chevy. I knew my parents wouldn't approve; I wasn't even allowed to date yet. But I figured what they didn't know wouldn't hurt me.

Unfortunately, my stepfather came home early that day and saw me in the car with Tom. He didn't follow me; he just went home and waited for me to return. I was 15 and a little old for a spanking, but that didn't stop him from hitting me very hard. He sent me to my room in tears and grounded me for a year. Yes, a full year. My mom thought the punishment was a little extreme, but she knew better than to go against his decisions. She took me to school and picked me up each day, and my brothers were told to report if I tried to so much as pick up the phone or step one foot outside our townhouse. That was the longest year of my life. It was also the beginning of the end of my relationship with my parents.

After that experience, I was desperate to become self-reliant. I didn't want to be dependent on my parents, and that included no longer working at their dry-cleaning business. So in July of 1967, I went out and looked for a summer job, and I found one—working as a receptionist at a dermatologist's office, in a building he shared with his brother, a dentist—that seemed great. But not everything is as it seems on the outside.

— COMMON THREAD —

If it's not what you were hired to do, get out.

At least I thought I was hired to be a receptionist. As it turned out, the dermatologist moved me to a back room in the suite of offices, and supplied me with a large cup of sharpened pencils and stacks of books containing statistical information on horse racing. Then he taught me to log racing statistics and create a racing handicap system.

One Friday afternoon, the doctor and his brother hosted a party in the dentist's office. The music was loud, everyone was drinking, and the party was getting more out of control by the minute. Before I realized what was happening, a man grabbed my arm and tried to pull me into the party. At first, everyone was laughing and joking that I was a stick-in-the-mud because I didn't want to come in. I continued to resist and at one point even clung to both sides of the doorjamb to keep from being pulled across the threshold. My efforts were in vain, and I was ushered into the party by a couple of middle-aged men.

I could hear a woman's voice yelling, "Find the key! Let's play find the key!" The men gathered around, and it was then that I realized that she was lying on the floor completely naked, daring the men to look in places not visible to the casual onlooker. In the meantime four men herded me into a corner in the restroom and were all urging me to take off my clothes and "play." The more they pushed, the more frightened I became. I kept telling them I was only 17, but they called me a liar as they pawed at me. Finally my boss came in and confirmed my age. Only then did the men begrudgingly let me go. I hurried back to my office, gathered my things, and left. I never went back.

— COMMON THREAD —

Every choice has a consequence.

It was my senior year in high school. We had recently moved and I was in a new school with no friends, and no encouragement for the future. I was exceedingly bitter about the move and was never allowed to express my unhappiness. The tension in our home in Long Beach was palpable, and as soon as I graduated from high school I left. Unfortunately, it was in the midst of a horrible fight with my mother.

It was only recently that I realized the impact this action had on others in my life. During a heated discussion with my youngest brother about our mother's health, he commented, completely out of the blue: "It all started when you packed up your shit and left when I was six. You never even talked to me about it before you left. One day you were my mom and the next day you were gone!"

— COMMON THREAD —

Get to know your spouse before— not after—you marry.

Part of the tension with my parents was caused by a relationship I had with an older man. We met while I was working after school at the family dry cleaners. His name was Vernon. He was 27, handsome, and a very smooth talker. I looked forward to seeing him whenever he dropped off his laundry, and I made it a point to spend time making small talk while I checked in his clothes. He finally asked me out to dinner one afternoon and when I told my parents who I was going out with, they were shocked. They tried to tell me how wrong it was to be interested in someone nine years older than me. After all, he had been married, was divorced, and already had a child! It was ridiculous! Their opinion might have held more weight had I not known that the age difference between my mother and birth father was 10 years and the age difference between my mother and my stepfather was the same. Their discouragement only fueled my desire to explore the mysteries of an older man. When I left home after a big blowup with my mom, the first place I went was to his apartment. That began a two-year off-and-on, live-in/move-out relationship.

Vernon had asked me to marry him, but I kept putting him off because my gut told me something was wrong. (Remember: If something feels wrong, it usually is.) Finally, when my grandfather made a comment that there was a "dark cloud" hanging over my head because I was "living in sin," the pleaser in me rose, and I told Vernon I would marry him. My grandfather may have been pleased, but my parents were devastated. The tears I saw in my mom and dad's eyes as I walked down the aisle weren't tears of joy, they were tears of despair. I had tried to please everyone but I ended up pleasing no one, not even myself.

Shortly after we were married I became pregnant. I had wanted to be a mom for as long as I could remember. I think it was because I wanted a chance to do things my way. I was the only one happy about the pregnancy. Vernon said he still had too much to do—hunting, fishing, and traveling. I insisted that having a child wouldn't stop any of those ambitions, and I spent the next several months feeling healthier and more in tune with myself then ever before. Unfortunately, I was also very much alone.

Troy was born in November 1970, and by the time he was 18 months old, it was clear my marriage was over. Troy's father had an affinity for alcohol and zero tolerance for noise, household clutter, meals not prepared in a timely manner, and a lack of sexual arousal. My becoming a new mom ran against the grain of everything he liked. I should have listened more closely to his ex-wife's comment when she heard I was pregnant: "That's too bad because he'll never have enough love to go around."

Vernon had always enjoyed his tequila and had come home from work drunk more than once. I recall one night when he staggered in the door at 11:30. When I asked, "Why didn't you call?" he launched into an angry diatribe about how he didn't need to check in with me. He followed me into the kitchen and picked up the thick, raw hamburger patty I was going to cook him when he got home. "What the hell is this!?" he yelled and then threw it at me. I ducked and it splattered against the wall, which led to both of us yelling.

Then I learned that just because you're married doesn't mean you can't be raped by your partner. Being forcefully pinned down to have sex against your will is the same in or out of wedlock. It happened late one night after Vernon came home from one of his frequent after-work stops with his friends. I knew at that moment I had to get out, but I was afraid of his temper. Flashbacks of my birth father beating my mother when he had been drinking reminded me of what could happen.

I spent the next few days going through the motions of being the perfect wife while soul searching about what I should do next. One morning, I kissed Vernon goodbye, told him to have a nice day at work, and within moments of his pulling out of the driveway gathered the bare necessities and loaded them into the old Rambler station wagon I drove. My heart was in my throat. I recall taking one fork, one spoon, one knife, one plate, one bowl, one glass, one cup, one pan, one towel, one washcloth, one can of tuna, and Troy's crib and clothes.

I was sick with fear as I drove to my mother's apartment to ask her to tend Troy while I found a place to live. I found a small place to rent month-to-month and quickly unloaded what little I had packed. The next day I set out to find a job.

Vernon hadn't wanted me to work after Troy was born, so I had been out of the job market for almost two years. The only marketable skill I'd learned in high school was typing, but fortunately there always seemed to be a secretarial or receptionist position available.

— COMMON THREAD —

Childhood prepares you for life, one way or another.

My mother was divorced by the time I was six, and one of the side effects of being a child of a single parent is that you tend to move a lot. In our case, we moved more than most, and in fact I attended four schools in the fourth grade alone. Every child internalizes that experience differently. The effect it had on me was that I became adept at fitting in quickly. I learned to prioritize and keep people at a distance. I learned not to make close friends because you would just have to leave them, and I learned how to be the head of the household by the time I was eight years old. All of those lessons gave me a great foundation for being a good employee. I always seemed to work for minimum wage, but I was able to figure out how to wring out an existence one way or another.

It had been over a year since I'd left Vernon. Although I was able to work the entire time, between childcare costs, doctor bills, and a long commute, I just couldn't get ahead. I needed to find a cheaper place to rent that was closer to my job. After an exhaustive search I finally found a one-bedroom apartment, which was actually an old garage. The owner had put up a couple of thin divider walls and installed a toilet and tiny sink and tub, all rust-stained from a drip that wouldn't stop. It also had a kitchenette that was so narrow I had to turn sideways facing the sink in order to slide in. It had a noisy, old refrigerator, and the small living room and bedroom were adorned with thin, frayed, stained carpet glued to the concrete floor. I put Troy's crib in the small bedroom and since I didn't have a bed or living-room furniture, I slept in an old leather chair that once belonged to my grandfather and a sleeping bag borrowed from my brother. This would be our new home for now.

Grocery money was scarce, and for a couple of months we ate pancakes for every meal. Fortunately, Troy was very young and thought it was fun to make funny shapes in the pan. To this day, I'm surprised he will still tolerate eating pancakes.

— COMMON THREAD —

Just because it's better doesn't make it good enough.

It was 1973, and I was working as a secretary at Fluor Corporation, just south of Los Angeles. Fluor engineered and built oil refineries all over the world. One day a field employee named Lou came in to take care of some expense forms. He had recently returned from an assignment in Saudi Arabia and was preparing for an assignment in Puerto Rico. He was funny and confident, and he asked me out to lunch a few times. We spent hours talking about his worldly travels and my lack thereof. We talked about family, and I learned he was divorced and had custody of his nine-year-old son, Scott, who was being raised by Lou's mother while Lou was overseas. I soon met the rest of his family and before we knew it, Lou was ready to leave for his next assignment.

The night before he left, he asked me to come with him to Puerto Rico and get married. I was caught off guard, since we had known one another for only a few weeks and things hadn't progressed past the kissing stage. He saw my surprise and asked, "How bad can it be? If it doesn't work out, you will have had one helluva vacation." I laughed it off and parted with the promise that I would think it over.

I put Troy to bed that night in the dilapidated converted garage with a cold draft creeping in through cracked windows. I crawled into the sleeping bag and tried to get comfortable on the chair. The sound of the dripping faucets seemed amplified, and the chugging of the old refrigerator seemed more annoying than ever. "How bad could it be?" it seemed to say. "How bad could it be?"

Within a couple of weeks, Lou was getting established in Ponce, Puerto Rico, and we were talking on the phone every night. He always ended the conversation with, "So, when are you coming down?" My typical response was laughter, but one night I said, "As soon as I can get my paperwork in order." There was a pregnant pause, and then he said, "Are you serious? Go see my mom and make arrangements to bring Scotty with you!"

It took two weeks to make the necessary arrangements, and against my parents' better judgment and Lou's mother's adamant objection to taking Scotty away from her, the three of us boarded a plane for a new adventure.

I spent the next several years perceived by some (one person in particular) as an evil stepmother. Scott's grandmother had spoiled him rotten, with few rules and with chocolate cake for breakfast. She'd finished his homework for him, thought if she disciplined him he wouldn't like her, and believed there was no such thing as a particular bedtime. None of these things were anywhere close to my standards for parenting, and if Scott was living with us he would have to live up to my standards.

Lou's job assignments typically lasted between 18 months and two years. We moved from Ponce, Puerto Rico, to Huntington Beach, California, to Alvin, Texas, south of Houston, where Justin was born in 1975. We then loaded up and moved to Edmonton, Alberta, Canada, then to Salt Lake City, Utah. I spent these years honing my skills of acclimating to one new place after another and finding a new job in each city.

We were supposed to be moving to Los Angeles from Edmonton but on the drive south we stopped in Salt Lake, where my parents had moved a few years earlier. My dad had finally given up on owning the family dry-cleaning business in southern California and had taken a job as a tailor with a regional men's clothing store based in Salt Lake. I suggested to Lou that he should continue on alone. The boys were showing the effects of changing schools frequently, and it was time to put down roots and give Scotty and Troy a chance to make some friends. If he wanted to stay married, he could finish the job in L.A. and then come join us to settle down in Salt Lake City.

The three boys and I stayed with my folks for the next six months while Lou worked in L.A. During that period I realized it was the first time since I'd been married to him that I was relaxed, happy, and at peace. I had to admit that it was because he wasn't around. His drinking had become more frequent over the past few years, and when he drank he became angry, loud, and abusive. I always seemed to be running interference between Lou, the boys, and anyone else around at the time. I knew it was a matter of time before I would have to make good on my threat to leave, but each time I brought up the situation, Lou was drinking and arguing and just not listening to what I was trying to say. When he arrived in Salt Lake, we bought a home and spent the next year trying to make things work.

— COMMON THREAD —

Buying a house together won't replace counseling.

Buying a house together didn't make all our problems disappear. In fact, they got worse. We argued about the bills, about the yard, about the kids and sometimes just argued to argue. Lou's drinking became a daily occurrence, his pride in his appearance and attitude disappeared, and his violent tendencies increased.

During the time we were married, Lou had lost one of his grandmothers along with his mother. He was harboring a grudge about Grandma Daisy leaving a small trust fund for the grandchildren but not leaving him a dime. Financial responsibility was not one of his long suits, and every time he would get in a bind he would ask his father for money. I didn't know this was happening until it came to light one night at dinner with his dad and his dad's new wife, Paula. Something started the conversation about Lou wanting to buy a new whatever and Paula said, "Why don't you just take care of yourself and stop asking your dad for money! Aren't you ever going to grow up?"

— COMMON THREAD —

Desperate people do desperate things.

I made a poor decision based on a desperate time in my life and although I gained a beautiful son and stepson, I could not make this marriage work. Lou was drinking more than ever, and the boys could sense the instability. He was also becoming more violent, and I was worried about the boys' safety. I decided to do the unthinkable and announce my intent to get a divorce at Christmas dinner, with Lou's father and the father's new wife present. Looking back, that probably wasn't the best way to handle the situation, but at that time I was afraid of what Lou would do if we were alone. Needless to say, the dinner ended early, the guests excused themselves, and Lou just kept drinking. I became "the bitch" in Lou and his father's eyes, and two months later on a Saturday morning, I packed up things for Troy and Justin and started moving out.

Lou had already begun with the Scotch the morning I started to pack. He came at me and in an instant I was pinned against the wall in the kitchen, dangling off the floor with Lou's hand around my throat. Just then Scott came in and pulled him off me, and I finished loading the car while every inch of me shook and I tried to fight back the tears. As I walked through the living room on the way out the door I saw Scott, sitting in a chair, with tears in his eyes. I went over to kiss him goodbye. He put his arms around my shoulders and pleaded, "Take me with you. Please!"

"I can't," I said. "You're dad is your legal guardian. I love you and I'll only be a phone call away, but I can't take you with me." Our hug lasted a long time, and he clung to me as I tried to break away.

It broke my heart to leave Scott there, knowing what was in store for him. Scott had become the cool big brother to both Troy and Justin. Once again, my actions affected so many more people than I had fully realized.

Days turned into weeks, then into months, and I could not stop thinking about my situation. What had I done wrong? How could I have made it better? Had I tried hard enough? Had I done everything I could have?

In the meantime, I was working and trying to provide some semblance of normalcy for the boys. Vernon had been out of Troy's life since he was three, Lou popped in and out to swoop Justin away for a Disneyland weekend, and Scott would drop by and visit occasionally.

— COMMON THREAD —

The desire to be desired causes temporary blindness.

At work it was different, and I was different. I was in control of my environment, was respected for what I accomplished, and people were happy to see me. Larry, one of the fabrication technicians, would stop by my desk occasionally to talk, and we would spend our lunch hours outside at the picnic table in mutual counseling sessions. He was going through a separation himself, and we compared notes about our failed relationships. It wasn't long before it became apparent we had a strong chemistry.

I was torn between what seemed to be a rebound reaction and a desperate need to be wanted. There was a less-than-ideal intimate side to my last marriage, and what started out as a belief that the sex didn't matter eventually grew into a deep feeling of emptiness. What Larry brought to the current situation was the long-lost idea of being desirable. It wasn't a feeling I had experienced in many years, and although hindsight would reveal that it was a shallow satisfaction, it seemed steeped with opportunity at the time. We began seeing one another, and within a year we were married. I moved into Larry's house with the boys and at first was ignorantly operating under the presumption that he owned it. Eventually I learned that the house was actually owned by his mother. This should have been a clue of what was to come, but sometimes we choose to ignore signs of reality.

— COMMON THREAD —

An apology doesn't erase the deed.

At first Larry seemed content with the life we were building together, but he quickly became possessive and jealous. He would get angry if I was five minutes late coming home from work and would become very territorial if either Troy or Justin wanted to be near me. He called them sissies and threatened them if they didn't stay away or "act like a man." That was another burning sign that something was terribly wrong, but I was so focused on not failing and making sure that this marriage didn't fall apart that I turned my head, to the detriment of my children. In the meantime, Larry had become less and less productive at work and more confrontational with his coworkers.

He was eventually fired from his job and was unemployed for more than a year. During that time, I tried to be a source of encouragement and pick up the load to make it easier for him. It seemed like the natural thing to do. Instead, all the while he grew angrier and more resentful, as well as abusive about my trying to "wear the pants in the family."

The situation I regret most is an evening when Larry and a friend were sitting at the table drinking beer and talking. I walked through the room, he made some crude remark, I responded, and the next thing I knew, he was out of his chair, yelling and shoving me into the living room. He never stopped yelling, and within seconds I tripped and he was kicking me into a corner. I was horrified to look up and see Troy and Justin standing at the end of the room, watching with terror on their faces and tears in their eyes. Larry's friend pulled him back and convinced him to go outside and cool off. I will never forget how humiliated I felt, how embarrassed I was, and what a lousy example of a parent I must have been at that moment.

What frightened me even more was learning, from a Report of the American Psychological Association Presidential Task Force on Violence and the Family, APA 1996, that a child who witnesses spousal abuse has a much higher risk of becoming violent him or herself.

That situation was just a precursor to others. One minute we would be sitting at the table talking and the next minute I would find myself ass-over-teakettle on the floor against the wall with my lip bleeding. Larry would immediately come over and tell me how sorry he was and promise not to hurt me again, as if the apology erased the action.

Looking back it was like being a porcelain vase on the table. Someone carelessly knocks it off one day, picks up the pieces, and glues it back together so it looks almost as good as new. After a while, however, the cracks are more visible and the small chips cannot be replaced. You even try to turn it around so the damage doesn't show. The next time it is knocked down and put back together another piece is gone, and soon there is a gaping hole that can't be ignored and can't be filled with anything else. That gaping hole was in my heart, and the rift in our relationship was getting larger and more evident every day.

— COMMON THREAD —

It's not always about you.

I was desperately trying not to fail again, and I even convinced Larry to go with me to marriage counseling. He would protest the entire time and not contribute a great deal. One Saturday morning after a counseling session I went out to the garage and found him sitting in his truck with a .45-caliber pistol in his hand. It terrified me. I tried to convince him to get out of the truck and put the gun away, that we would work things out. He said there was nothing left to talk about and he put the barrel of the gun in his mouth. I was crying and begging him to put it down; he put the gun in his lap and began to back his vehicle out of the garage. He said he was going to just go someplace and kill himself. I went back in the house in tears and tried to figure out what I had done to cause him to want to commit suicide.

Late that night he came home and climbed into bed in silence. I felt like I was drowning. There seemed to be no bottom, nothing I could grab onto, and I was exhausted. I looked around for help, but it seemed as if everything and everyone was too far away. At times it felt as though it would just be easier to give up, to keep sinking; surely there was a bottom someplace. Then I would think about the boys and what they were going through, and it tore at my heart. It wasn't their fault or their fight, and they were depending on me to take care of them.

The next day I called our counselor. I explained how I was feeling alone and exhausted and told her about the incident with the gun. Her response was, "Larry has handed you a boa constrictor and it's squeezing the life out of you. You need to hand it back." She recommended that the next time he threatened suicide, "Tell him you are very sorry he feels that way but it's not your fault and then take the kids and get out." Easy for her to say; she had not come to know the deep-seated Pleaser in me yet.

— COMMON THREAD —

What others don't know can hurt you.

One lesson I learned when I divorced Lou was that it doesn't pay to keep the negatives to yourself. When you keep your problems hidden, and you've finally reached your limit and decide to do something about it, no one knows you have ever had an unhappy moment, and your friends and family think you just woke up one day and decided to leave. Although it is difficult to share negative feelings with your family, you must do it for your sake and the sake of your relationship.

While I hadn't told my parents and coworkers everything that had been going on with Larry, they knew it wasn't paradise around our house. One clue may have been when Larry decided to sit in the parking lot of the office building where I worked and watch me through the windows—for hours at a time. Another may have been when I came to work with a split lip and a six-foot stuffed bear was delivered to my desk by noon that day. A coworker lent some clarity to my situation one day when I said, "I just don't want to fail again." He thought for a moment and then responded, "Failure is knowing there is a problem you can fix and doing nothing. Success is having the courage to do something about it." When I called my stepfather and asked him if I could bring the boys and come to stay at their house, he knew something major had occurred. Historically I have been a very proud, even stubborn person, and the last thing I would ever do is ask for help. The vase had been knocked off the table one too many times, and it could no longer hold water.

— COMMON THREAD —

It's just stuff.

A few days after I moved in with my parents, I contacted Larry. I told him I wasn't coming home but I wanted to come pick up our things. We arranged a time and I asked my brother to accompany me; needless to say I was afraid of what might happen. My brother came by my parents' house with one of his very large friends named James, who would put the fear of God in just about anyone. (Truth be known, he was actually the most gentle spirit you could ever meet.) We drove over to the house and found several green trash bags out on the lawn with Larry standing next to them, holding that familiar .45-caliber gun in his hand. Ah, yes...the amicable separation we all hope for.

By the end of the two-month stretch of bunking with my parents, I had saved enough money to move into an apartment. I had unloaded only a few of the green trash bags I had picked up off the lawn. Once we were in the bare apartment, we opened the remaining bags to find that Larry's mother had helped him gather things they felt we deserved. The bags with the boys' clothes also contained dirt and lint from the floor and under their beds. I have a searing memory of Justin looking at me through tear-filled eyes and saying, "Mom, we don't have any of our *stuff*—what are we going to do?" That was when we had the "it's only stuff" talk and I assured the boys that as long as we had each other, we would be just fine. We could always get more stuff.

— COMMON THREAD —

You learn what you live.

Following my divorce and a fairly long stretch without dating, I finally decided to allow myself to be a little vulnerable and be open to some male companionship. It seemed that I kept being drawn to a particular type of person—someone who initially liked me for my independence but was soon intimidated by my strength. When things began to get a little rocky, I always fell back to the childhood "it must be something I'm doing wrong" theory. I would have long talks with myself and try and be as objective and honest as possible. I would analyze the process and try and figure out what went wrong, then promise myself that I wouldn't make that mistake again. Time after time, it seemed as though something just didn't fit.

I finally became so frustrated that I sought the help of a professional. I found a psychiatrist who came highly recommended, but I was cautioned that he was a little pricey. Trying to get by on my secretary's salary, I thought twice before making the appointment, but the long talks in my own head weren't helping. I felt terribly lost and knew I needed a professional point of view.

Here I was, the strong, self-directed, confident woman who was viewed by friends and coworkers as having it all together, waiting to be analyzed by a shrink! Needless to say, I hadn't mentioned it to anyone but my mother prior to making the appointment because as everyone knows, you don't see a shrink unless you yourself are a little "woo-woo," as my mom would say.

A man walked through the door with an outstretched hand and introduced himself as the psychiatrist. He reminded me of Elmer Fudd, right down to his height, plaid shirt, corduroy pants, and bald head. How was I supposed to maintain any sort of composure when I was being interviewed by a cartoon character? It took some self-control, but soon after the discussions began, "Elmer" dissolved into a warm, intuitive, get-to-the-point professional. I began our meeting by telling him that I had limited funds and that I suggested he take copious notes because I planned to talk very fast. I was pleasantly surprised by his intelligent questions and his insightful responses to my answers.

Together we peeled away the layers to the beginning of my life and worked our way forward. It took six visits before I had that coveted "ah-ha!" moment. It came after some revealing discussions about my birth father. My revelation was that just because my father did something or said something, it didn't make it so. What he believed wasn't necessarily correct. For 40 years I had functioned subconsciously believing that accepting the actions and words of my father was like breathing—it just happened. It was just a part of life. I discovered that what I had been taught was wrong. Not questioning "why" was wrong. Accepting abuse was wrong. Living in fear of rejection was wrong. I had been taught to be a Pleaser. My mother's example was based purely on fear; it reflected an effort to minimize collateral damage. As a small child all I saw was Mommy always helping, always doing for others, always trying to anticipate my father's every need. It is no surprise that I grew up being the Pleaser just like my mom. This title comes with a great deal of self-sacrifice and lack of self-respect. No one ever explained that sacrifice should be a choice, not a given. Being a martyr is overrated, and is destructive to your self-image and to those around you. Like the flight attendant always tells us as we prepare to take off on a plane, first put your own mask on; then help others around you.

chapter two

You're Not Alone

Courage is fear that has said its prayers.
DOROTHY BERNARD

W hen I determined that I wanted to follow my story with that of another individual who had experienced domestic violence and come through it a better person, I knew it would be difficult to find someone. Not because there aren't many women who have experienced some sort of abuse and lack of self-respect, but because most of us don't talk about it. Sadly, statistics show we're certainly not alone. Studies by the Surgeon General's office reveal that domestic violence is the leading cause of injury to women between the ages of 15 and 44, more common than automobile accidents, muggings, and cancer deaths combined. Other research, cited in the *Journal of the American Medical Association* in 1990, has found that half of all women will experience some form of violence from their partners during marriage, and that more than one-third are battered repeatedly every year.

Asking my friends whether they knew anyone who'd be willing to tell her story proved to be an effort in futility. I went to my local YWCA website, because I knew they housed a center for abused women and children. From there I learned about a newly instituted program called the Speak for Success Women's Leadership Institute. The program was founded by Dana Bristol-Smith in 2007, and they had just graduated their first class of participants in June 2008. I reached out to Dana, and she put Lana in touch with me within a day.

Lana's brief introductory email gave me a glimpse into some of the challenges she had overcome. As a child, she heard her mom being shot by her dad while she lay in bed. Her history included rape, multiple pregnancies, drug addiction, personal abuse, and divorce.

We met at a Starbucks and had she not sent me her photo prior to our meeting, I certainly would not have been able to pick her out of the crowd. Lana is an attractive young blond woman with sparkling eyes and a confident smile. She shook my hand firmly. We found a place to sit, and she asked where she should start. I responded, "At the beginning."

This is Lana's story.

Meet Lana Culliver

Lana was born in a very small town in Alabama in 1968. Lana's mom was 17. Her dad started a trucking company, like his father before him, and it became a fairly successful business. Her recollection of her early childhood was that it was simply "enchanted." She didn't have many friends and although she had two younger brothers, she spent a great deal of time alone.

— COMMON THREAD —

Stress can be deadly.

When she was eight years old, Lana's parents decided to move to a big city in Florida and build a beautiful new home. That's when her life took a horrible turn. It was as if the move to the city turned on the switch for domestic violence. Her parents argued almost daily, both during the construction of the house and once they'd moved in. Her dad drank more frequently and the violence escalated; she recalls pretending to be sick in order to try and create an excuse for her parents to stop fighting.

One night, when she was nine, she went to bed to the sounds of her parents arguing and was awakened by a loud noise. At first she tried to go back to sleep but when she heard a lot of commotion, she went downstairs. Her dad was drunk, her mother was lying in a pool of blood, and he was insisting on driving her to the hospital. Lana remembers being terribly frightened, knowing something very bad had just happened but not understanding exactly what was going on. The next thing she remembers is the police arriving at their home and an officer trying to pry the mop out of her hands. She was attempting to clean up the blood from the shiny new kitchen floor because she was worried her mom would be angry.

Her mother survived the gunshot wound, and during the next three years, she moved in and out of the pretty new house. Although her parents divorced, they repeatedly tried to make their relationship work. The environment was very unstable, very confusing for a child, and it distanced Lana from her enchanted life more each day. She was feeling increasingly rejected, unloved, and alone. The summer that Lana was eleven, her mom took the children and moved out for good.

Starving for attention is hazardous to your health.

At the same time that Lana was starving for attention, she also began noticing boys. She was headed for the perfect storm. One fall evening, she sneaked out of the apartment to meet a 17-year-old boy, and they began to get friendly. All she could think was, *Someone likes me!* What began as her efforts to be a Pleaser ended in rape. She was so frightened and embarrassed at the time that she didn't tell anyone what had happened. She eventually told a friend, the friend told her parents, and her parents told Lana's mom. By the time the story got back to her home, all her mom heard was that her wayward daughter had had sex. Lana remembers having a terrible fight with her mom, and her mom screaming that she would kill her if she brought home any diseases. She made Lana bathe in a horrible combination of household cleaners, including Lysol and bleach, and made her feel like the scourge of the earth. That was the start of Lana's mom treating her as if she was the source of whatever problems were happening at the time, not to mention influencing her view of sex (forcible or consensual) at the young age of eleven.

Lana became more and more anxious and shy, and social situations were very painful. When she was a senior in high school, she met a 25-year-old man who would change the way she felt. He lavished her with gifts, gave her a great deal of attention, and made all sorts of promises, one of which was that they would get married. All of this was in exchange for sex, although that is not how Lana saw it at the time. She just knew that she was accepted and "loved," and that was all that mattered. When she thought she was pregnant, her boyfriend went to the doctor's office with her to confirm her suspicions. When the test came back positive, his first words were, "Well, that really messes up my grad school plans. When are you getting an abortion?"

Lana wasn't particularly religious at the time, but she had strong reservations about abortion. Her boyfriend's badgering, however, led her to go through with the procedure—ironically enough, on the day that *Roe vs. Wade* became law.

He went on to grad school in Mississippi and she went on to the University of South Alabama, majoring in English. They remained engaged, and Lana would often drive to Mississippi State University to visit him. Distance had not made their hearts grow fonder, however; in fact it was quite the opposite. She heard through the grapevine that her fiancé had been sleeping with other girls, and that was enough of an excuse for her to break off the engagement and date other young men. At the age of 20, she once again became pregnant.

Lana and the baby's father had become close, but once the new boyfriend's father heard the news, he sent his son a plane ticket and he was out of her life. This time she was pregnant and alone. Lana was feeling lost and abandoned and recalls the example set by her grandparents, who were very strong Catholics with steadfast morals and beliefs. That memory drove her to contact the Catholic Adoption Services. She began the adoption process, and when she delivered the baby and handed it over, "it felt like my heart was ripped out." She was able to stay in touch with the family, but she felt very lonely and craved a child of her own.

By the time Lana was 21, she was pregnant yet again. She met this man when she was alone, depressed, and vulnerable. He was the perfect listener, and seven months later they were married. This time she was determined to make the relationship work. They both had jobs, they rented a house together, and everything seemed great. Little did she know that she had married a drug dealer and the person who would become her abuser.

Lana was working for a company that provided Section 8 housing, and on a trip to the local military base one day to post the housing notices she had an "ah-ha!" moment. She observed all the people in uniform, everyone scurrying about looking responsible and important, and thought, "I want to be like them. I want to join the military!"

Her husband, Vincent, agreed to care for their son, Chance, and Lana's mom picked him up almost every weekend. Lana was off to join the Navy, and as she headed for boot camp, she believed she had finally found her career path. She wanted to become a military linguist, specializing in Arabic. Her training would take her to Monterey, California. The course was demanding and only 30 people out of the original 70 completed it; she was one of them.

Two years into her military career, Lana gave birth to another son. Things seemed to be going well. Although her husband never became entrenched in a particular career path, he always seemed to have the money they needed. She realized that most things had to be his way, but they were happy, and that was all that mattered to her.

— COMMON THREAD —

Always have a Plan B.

Almost five years into her career, Lana was taking a standard battery of vaccine shots when she had a very bad reaction to the typhoid injection. She was eventually given a medical discharge. This was an enormous disappointment, as the military was supposed to be her life's work. She'd had direction and purpose, and now she had nothing.

Lana became pregnant for a fifth time when she was still out of work. She had voiced her concerns about their finances with her husband, and he had become increasingly irritated and ultimately abusive. He decided they should move back to Pensacola, Florida, his hometown. Lana was too intimidated to object, though she had a bad feeling about the move. It was no surprise to her when the marriage began to go downhill fast. Her husband used drugs more frequently, and the abuse escalated. She was unusually ill with her pregnancy, and when the doctor did an ultrasound examination, he confirmed that she was pregnant with fraternal triplets!

During one of her husband's drug-induced rants, he pushed Lana against a wall and kicked her, which resulted in the loss of two of her babies. She was filled with anger, guilt, and self-doubt, and his verbal attacks were adding to her emotional distress. In the midst of all the chaos, they decided to buy a house. It was the biggest, nicest house on the block, and they were the envy of the neighborhood. The women who came over to the house as "friends" ended up being drug users who were also bed partners to her husband. And yet, from the outside, people thought they were the perfect family. After all, everyone thought Vincent was so likeable!

In 2001, Lana's only daughter was born. Lana had gone back to work and back to school but was having a major problem concentrating. She was diagnosed with adult attention deficit disorder, and her doctor prescribed Adderall. Suddenly everything was clear. She explained, "It was like driving in the rain without windshield wipers and then turning them on—Wow! Everything was crystal clear!" Lana changed jobs and had no insurance for a while, so her doctor prescribed a less expensive drug, Ritalin. She went from focused to fixated. One of her "friends" showed her how to crush the drug and snort it. When her husband found out, he introduced her to cocaine. In Lana's words, "It hijacked my life."

In 2003 during one of their fights, her husband almost ran over her, intentionally. The next day, she and the kids moved out. They spent the next year essentially homeless, moving approximately 20 times. Lana went on a two-year binge: drinking, using, and taking risks with the kids. Between 2003 and 2005, they moved from Florida to Alabama to Mississippi and then back to Florida. One night she had hit the bottom of her life and called her estranged husband. She told him she was seriously "messed up" and asked him to come to the hotel, pick up the kids, and take the drugs she had in her purse. He did, but came back to the hotel later, loaded on the drugs he had taken from her purse, and begged her to join him on his drug-induced high and get back together.

Against everything her gut was telling her, Lana agreed to try and work things out. Their "perfect house" was nearing foreclosure, but Vincent made the delinquent payments and they all moved back in just before Christmas. They had no furniture, just the clothes on their backs, a small Christmas tree, and some gifts for the kids. It wasn't long before Vincent brought home some cocaine, they both got loaded, he got violent, and this time he almost killed her. She recalls going in and out of consciousness, feeling him kicking and punching her and at one point, almost drowning her. She drove herself to the hospital and at first refused to tell the doctor what had happened. She finally admitted her addiction and abuse, and the doctor encouraged her to end her relationship. She went home to split up with her husband, but they instead got back together again. The lure of the drugs was just too strong. Her husband was eventually arrested for buying drugs. He went to jail and when he came out, he said he was a changed man. He then proceeded to get high and violent again.

— COMMON THREAD —

We change only when the pain is great enough.

Lana knew she would have to move out and stay out. She had no money in the bank but had just received her final unemployment check, so she gathered up the children, rented a condo on the beach, and pretended they were on vacation for a month. All the while, she was getting loaded. She said she could feel her spirit dying more every day. She sent her oldest son to live with his dad and dropped the next two children off with her estranged husband. She took her daughter, went to the bus terminal, and purchased two tickets to San Diego (as far away from her husband as she could afford). With the money left in her pocket, she boarded the bus with her little girl and kept thinking to herself, *The Lord knows I am trying this time; he will help me.*

When Lana arrived in San Diego, she found the Rescue Mission and got in line for a holiday lunch. "I remember thinking, I wasn't even in town three hours and already the mayor was serving me lunch! That must mean something good is going to happen, right?" They were able to stay in the shelter for three nights, then moved to a hotel for two weeks, and finally got into the YWCA program, where she could begin to put her life back together. She spent four months in transitional housing, then moved into a V.A. transitional housing program, then to St. Vincent de Paul for eight months. In the meantime she found a job.

In April of 2006, Lana sent for her two younger sons, and in June 2007 she sent for her oldest son. Two years from her initial stay at the YWCA, she moved into her own apartment. She is gainfully employed, all her children are doing well, and once again she's happy. She said that although all the changing and moving was difficult, it made her family stronger. Going through the Speak for Success program changed her life and helped her to realize that her life lessons have been a gift. She has learned to speak up, to set goals, and to explore her lifelong question of "why am I here?" She has discovered that part of the answer lies in her desire to help people. She also knows how important it is to teach some priceless lessons to her children—lessons about individual values, self-respect, and never settling, no matter how old you are.

Lana has reached out with her advice. In November 2008, she posted the first official blog entry on behalf of the Speak for Success program. Her goal is to connect with other women who may have had or are currently experiencing some type of abuse and provide them with encouragement and hope. Her web address is *www.speakforsuccess.com*.

Lana didn't have a specific person or support circle of friends or family she could turn to for unconditional love and help if needed. Find someone you can trust—a mentor, a friend, an extended family member, or a small or large group of friends who will make the commitment to watch out for one another. Check in on a regular basis and share the good times and the bad, knowing you won't be judged. We all need someone who cares about us, no matter what is happening in our lives. Find someone and be that someone.

chapter three

Dream Beyond Your Genes

*One can never consent to creep
when one feels an impulse to soar.*

HELEN KELLER

Our genes are the common threads eternally woven through our families for generations.

True or False: Your genetics determine your future. In order to answer this question accurately, you probably should have been given a third choice: *Sort of.*

My mother was born in a small town in southern Utah. The landscape surrounding the town was (and still is) red rock plateaus, deep green winding rivers, tall majestic spruce, clusters of white bark cottonwood trees, and fat brown-and-white cattle grazing on acres of fenced meadows. The summer skies were blue and the breezes were hot; the winters were dusted with shimmering snow, and spring green was a color of its own. She and six of her brothers and sisters were brought into this world by a Native American Indian midwife named La Wana, and they were all born in the red brick house my grandfather built for my grandmother before they were wed. It was the only house they would know until they moved away when my mother was a teenager.

Fast forward to my birthplace: Los Angeles, California. Nothing but concrete freeways, tall gray buildings, and two seasons—summer and fog. My mom was divorced by the time I was six, I moved four times while in the fourth grade, and we never lived in a house we owned until I was 15.

It's important to know about your heritage, your family health history, and the way your parents and their parents were brought up; after all, we learn what we live. We are all born with a blank slate as far as life experiences are concerned, and the only point of reference we are given is that of our parents or the people who raised us.

Before we are even able to focus our eyes we begin to develop our own set of "life lenses," based on our environment. We develop our own perception of what a family looks and sounds like, what our belief systems and work ethics are, and how our dietary habits and educational values are formed. Much of what we learn is never intentionally taught or spoken but rather felt or observed, and for many years we don't know that all children aren't raised exactly the same way we are. With every word, action, and reaction, we are all subconsciously imprinted by our surroundings.

There is a certain time in your life when you determine (consciously or subconsciously) that you actually have reasoning skills and the ability to make up your own mind. That's the good news and the bad news. You may arrive at some of your conclusions through common sense or the avoidance of physical pain or emotional turmoil. You develop other perceptions through observing and talking with your family, friends, or teachers. This all leads to the formation of your own personal acceptance code.

At a very young age most of us begin to hear things like "she got that from her mom/dad/grandmother...she's so smart, so stubborn, so athletic," et cetera. Unfortunately, as a child most of us don't understand that although we may have inherited some attributes, we aren't stuck with an inherited attitude, a will to succeed or fail, or a passion to make a difference in the world around us. Even though we may have inherited some tendencies, we have a choice about our attitude and about the types of people we surround ourselves with, and those decisions will affect every other opportunity we have in the years to come.

In contrast to me, my mom was raised in a large family with strong work ethics and strong ties to the Mormon Church (Church of Jesus Christ of Latter Day Saints, or LDS). In fact, her maternal grandmother was among the first Mormon pioneers who pulled hand carts across the treacherous trails from Illinois to Utah to escape religious persecution. She and her closest brother were the only two of eight siblings who made life choices based on a burning desire to rebel against those religious beliefs. What she passed on to me was a strong work ethic, a lack of faith in the LDS Church, a propensity for abusive relationships, a tendency toward breast cancer and divorce, a fierce stubborn streak, my birth father's brown eyes, a love affair with southern Utah, and a positive attitude. No wonder it's taken me a while to get straightened out.

The opportunity to choose your path is a glorious gift! Along that path are forks in the road, and you need to choose your direction over and over again. Each decision comes with consequences; some are positive and some are less than desirable. We have all had our share of opportunities to be in a place that was less than desirable and to turn it into something valuable.

One of the ramifications of making decisions and trying new things is that you will inevitably encounter challenges. Since I'm a very visual thinker, I tend to sort my challenges into small, medium, and large sizes and put them into colored boxes in my mind. (Don't laugh—it works for me.) I visualize all the boxes having lids and if I can't find a solution for something or overcome a challenge at that moment, I put it in a box and close the lid. I will always have a variety of boxes in my mind, and I find a strange sense of control knowing I don't have to deal with everything at once—I can choose to handle my various challenges when I'm ready. If I solve a problem, I mentally file the positive lessons I learned and the problem simply goes away. If I can't solve it at that moment, it goes back in the box until I have more information or time to deal with it. How many boxes would you have stacked in your mind if you were to put your challenges in boxes right now? Starting out it might be easier if you write them all down, sort from large to small, and *then* put them in boxes—or not. At least now, you can see what you're dealing with.

As I grew older and took on more responsibilities, my challenges changed. There has never been a time in my life when my mind was clear of boxes—that would mean I had no more dreams or goals or challenges. In a very philosophical way, it is comforting to know I have a lot to work on, accomplish, or experience. It's what fills that half-asleep, half-awake time first thing in the morning.

Why is all this relevant? Because your ability to explore your past, examine your current situation, and dream big will bring rewards you would probably not have imagined otherwise. A poignant example of this is one woman who made a conscious choice not to follow her genes.

When I decided to ask Diana if she would be willing to be a part of my book, she responded with a big smile, "I'd be honored!" We met at her modest home in an established neighborhood in San Diego. Just inside the short white wrought-iron gate, Diana's front yard was filled with a collection of containers, each with a plant at a different stage of health. When I entered the house, she proudly guided me through her home. Diana was almost embarrassed about all of the remodel work she had done, but explained that since her recent near-death experience, she had determined that she would "take life by the horns" and enjoy it while she could.

As Diana began her story, it was clear that she did indeed dream beyond her genes. When she was finished, she suggested that I use a fictitious name because she didn't want people she knew to learn about the dark side of her life. I convinced her that her path was one that would inspire even more young women if they knew who she was and how far she had truly come.

Meet Diana Venable

The train bound for Philadelphia was so crowded and noisy that none of the other passengers noticed that tears streamed down Diana's tiny face. Since she was only six years old, Diana knew only a part of what had gone on when living with her mother in a run-down shanty in Waukegan, Illinois. It wasn't much of a life, but it was all she'd ever known, and she didn't want to leave.

What she didn't know or understand was that her mother had conceived a child with someone other than her father. Within a few months, her father was shipped out to the Aleutian Islands and while he was away, her mother had given birth. When her father came home on leave, he was excited to be reconnected with his wife. But once he learned that truth about the baby, he divorced her mother and returned to his military post. What he did not know was that during the brief time they had reunited, he had fathered his own child, Diana. This began Diana's life with a single mom who couldn't seem to exist without having a man under her roof, and it usually was not the same man for long. Diana's childhood memories were haunted by the shrieking of angry voices, the nauseating smell of stale alcohol, and the gnawing fear that nothing was secure. The most recent man in her mother's life had convinced her to send Diana away to live with her father, a man Diana had never met. During that lonely and terrifying train ride, Diana knew one thing for certain—she never wanted to be like her mother.

When she finally arrived at her destination she was hungry, tired, and nervous. Much to her surprise and relief, she was greeted at the train station by a very tall, handsome man who scooped her up in his arms and gave her a warm hug. He took her home to meet his wife, who Diana later endearingly referred to as "Mommy."

Diana's stepmother was a teacher, and her father had become a brilliant research chemist. He never stopped pursuing his education and at the age of 44, he graduated from Massachusetts Institute of Technology summa cum laude with a doctorate in Infrared Spectroscopy.

Despite her father's professional status, their African-American heritage and the associated social dictates of the 1950s and '60s relegated them to a poor section of Philadelphia. Yet where they lived didn't affect *how* they lived. Their home was modest but always well maintained, clean, and filled with love and lots of books.

Some of Diana's friends, however, didn't share her lifestyle or the principles instilled by her father and stepmother. She watched many of her peers succumb to lives of crime and academic underachievement. From this experience she learned to be street smart as well as book smart, which in adult life enabled Diana to bridge the huge social, cultural, and economic gap among the people she befriended.

— COMMON THREAD —

Value is relative.

Diana learned some valuable lessons at an early age. Sometimes she watched with curiosity through the window as a man dressed in tattered, stained clothes rummaged through trash cans along her street. One Sunday afternoon her family took a drive through a wealthy suburb, admiring the large, well-manicured homes. As they drove, she spotted the same tattered man, but now he was dressed in clean, pressed trousers and a white shirt and was selling his wares to the residents of the suburb. That was when she first realized that the concept of value is subject to individual interpretation.

Diana's father oversaw a strict but loving home, and she excelled in an all-girls high school and graduated with honors at the age of 16. She realized that she was blessed with a long line of very intelligent relatives on her father's side, and gaining an education had come naturally to her. Bright and resourceful, she received her bachelor's degree from Temple University and then pursued a master's in accounting. She became a CPA by the time she was 22.

She explored the idea of working for one of the large firms in her area or maybe moving to someplace like Boston or New York. Then it came to her. What she needed was a change—a big change. Her ongoing college success had filled her with confidence and opened her mind to all sorts of possibilities. Diana made a spontaneous decision to go to Los Angeles. Although she had never been west of the Mississippi, she had read about all the opportunities that were just waiting to be snatched up. Within two weeks she sold everything she owned except her car and headed for the excitement of L.A. Although she didn't know anyone there, Diana was sure she could find employment, and just the thought of starting a new adventure gave her butterflies. Success was calling her name.

Once she arrived in L.A., the sobering facts seemed bigger than life and reality didn't look anything like the vision she had created in her mind. The people were all in a hurry, the countryside was covered with concrete freeways and tall gray buildings, and it was noisy, very noisy. After a few weeks of job rejections, sleepless nights, and getting out of bed only to find bugs scurrying out from under her feet, she headed for Marin County, an area a little farther north and a little less crowded. There was more greenery along the roadside but no better work opportunities. Diana was determined not to fail. She swallowed her pride and moved back to Los Angeles a short time later.

She spent the next eight years working in the accounting department at what is now the King-Drew Medical Center. Her strong work ethic and frugal financial practices enabled her to purchase a new car, and she decided to buy something special—a Jaguar! But she worked in Watts, a very poor community that had just experienced explosive riots, looting, and mass destruction. The population was still angry and filled with resentment, and

Diana's nice car was overturned more than once while she worked there. She finally decided she needed a change.

In 1976 she moved south to San Diego, California. On the drive down the coast she reflected on her past, her family, and her path. It made her sad to think that out of the seven children her mother bore, only she and one brother had been able to break the chain of poverty and realize their potential.

Diana secured a position as head accountant at National Pump and Injector. She managed a staff of 22 people and she continued her education by going to classes on government contracts. However, the company she worked for was led by a father and son, and it soon became apparent to Diana that no matter what her experience or education was, she would never be given the opportunity to rise to the top. They would always try and keep the more lucrative responsibilities within the family.

— COMMON THREAD —

Pursue your passion.

Diana enjoyed shopping for antiques and over the years had educated herself on what was valuable. In 1979 she purchased a cabin in a small mountain town called Julian, about an hour's drive outside San Diego, and frequented garage sales to secure all the furniture and trappings needed to make it feel like home. She ended up purchasing far more than she could ever use or store in the cabin, so she decided to quit her job and pursue her passion—antiques and collectibles. She took part of her grocery money and went to swap meets five days a week. Between her buying and selling, she was able to eke out a living. Diana took a position with an estate liquidator for a short time, and in March of 1985, along with putting her CPA training to good use by establishing a tax preparation service, she began her own estate liquidation business. When she started, there were four competing companies in the San Diego area; by 2006 there were 104. Despite the increased competition, if you asked her how business was doing she would smile and tell you, "It's great!" She could choose which clients to work for, decide what her hours would be, and do what she loved.

When I asked Diana about her many successes in life, she told me about a day when she was working in her garden and heard a soft voice from behind the fence. "Hello? Hello?" She ignored it, but again she heard, "Hello." She didn't answer and retreated into the house. The Japanese family who had recently moved in next door was a reminder of Pearl Harbor, and she still felt a great deal of anger. She sat quietly in her living room and confronted herself out loud: "What are you doing? He's just a child!" The little boy was about seven and she had seen him playing with marbles in his yard. She had amassed a wonderful collection of rare marbles and decided that it was the only "peace offering" that would be worthy of her shameful actions. She gathered them up and went back out to the fence. She told him, "Hi, I heard you like marbles. Maybe you would like these." He accepted and they began a loving, healing, mentoring relationship that would last for many years to come.

One day while Diana was helping the little boy with his homework, he told her he didn't understand why he had to work so hard. After all, he would never graduate from high school anyway. She asked why he thought that. He explained that his mother talked to a fortune teller who told her that her last-born child wouldn't finish high school. He was the last-born child. This made no sense to Diana, and she set out to do whatever it took to encourage him to study and follow through with his education. She refers to the day she sat in the audience and watched him receive his diploma as her proudest moment ever.

Many of Diana's neighbors were struggling immigrants and the working poor, and she "adopted" dozens of kids and became a member of their families. She acted as a role model, mentor, confidante, and benefactor. Although she never had any children of her own, many of her "kids" went on to become doctors, lawyers, and successful businessmen and women. As a tribute to Diana, they all lovingly call her "Mom."

Diana was always determined not to be like her birth mother. In hindsight, she said, the best thing her mother ever did was to put her on that train when she was six. Throughout her life she had many good friends, but it was not until the age of 44 that one special person asked for her hand in marriage and she finally accepted. Within a year she was divorced, and she explained, "He thought that once we were married, he had me where he wanted me and it just wasn't where I wanted to be!" She realized that she didn't need someone else in her life to make her whole and she was not willing to forfeit her own potential to accommodate someone else's.

When it comes to relationships or career choices, Diana believes that when you are at a crossroads or feel lost or unfulfilled, "Follow your passion. Reach for the stars and be willing to sacrifice and work hard for what you want." To younger women, she urges, "Stay in school. Get as much education as you can and then apply it to your dreams."

— COMMON THREAD —

What goes around comes around.

In late 2004, Diana developed a bacterial infection in her eye that almost killed her. The doctors couldn't pinpoint how she'd contracted the bug but surmised that it could have come from a scratch she received while playing with her dog. She made many trips to the emergency room in excruciating pain before the doctors finally had no choice but to surgically remove her eye in order to save her life. During that time the friends she had made around the community and in the Rotary Club were by her side, night and day, holding her hand, encouraging her and just letting her know she was loved. They gave back to her all of the selfless sacrifices she had made over the years.

When she believed she was going to die, she gave a lot of thought to how she had lived her life and how she wanted to be remembered. "I would just like people to remember me for what I tried to demonstrate: the art of fairness, tolerance, patience, sharing, and generosity."

Diana eventually recovered from her eye surgery and was excited to become active in her community again. Unfortunately, not long after her recovery from the bacterial infection, Diana died unexpectedly from an apparent heart attack on June 24, 2006. The headline in the local paper above her lengthy, loving obituary read, "Diana Venable, 59; volunteer made city a better place to live."

Within the next two years, her friends in Rotary established a scholarship foundation in Diana's name. Diana's belief in the importance of a good education will be passed along to deserving young people for many years to come, and she is a perfect example of how your genes don't need to determine your destiny.

chapter four

Write Your Plan in Pencil

Someday change will be accepted as life itself.

SHIRLEY MacLAINE

I t seems as though we are all looking for an edge, an advantage, or some sort of guidance to help make our journey down life's path an enriched one.

— COMMON THREAD —

Writing it makes it real.

In 1993, I was becoming more and more comfortable being a single parent and spending time with myself and my boys; after all, I had been single for nine years at that point and it was getting easier by the day. I had finally realized that I had been looking at my life as a big puzzle and, even though I was happy with the picture it was creating, was incomplete. I'd believed that "someone" was the missing piece to my unfinished puzzle. Now I began to see that I am the only one who can find the right pieces to complete the puzzle.

During that same time, a friend suggested I read a book entitled *Are You the One for Me?* written by Barbara De Angelis. The book was intended for people who had experienced a challenge in establishing positive relationships, and it included tools to help partners gain clarity on their individual needs and expectations. At the end of the book there was an exercise that asked readers to make a list of their preferences for the perfect partner. Not only were you to list specific traits, but you were to go into detail about exactly what those traits looked like. Some of the items for consideration were appearance, sense of humor, education, interests, religion or spirituality preferences, sexual preferences, and sensitivities. I figured it would be fun and interesting to complete the list and see what my perfect partner would look like, inside and out. My greatest challenge was to be totally honest with each trait and write down what I wanted and not what I thought other people would expect me to want. This list was for the reader's eyes only, and the author suggested writing it in pencil because in reality, your needs change over time. You were also to refer to the list often to remind yourself what "the perfect partner" looked like.

The following year I became friends with a man named Art who had moved into an office building I was managing in Salt Lake City. Several months into our friendship, he stopped by my office on a Friday afternoon and I asked him casually, "So do you have any plans for the weekend?" He said he needed some "think time" and was going to drive south to Monument Valley. He surprised me by asking if I wanted to tag along. All I was expected to bring was a sleeping bag, so I went along for the adventure.

We drove for most of the night and slept in the car for a few hours before reaching our final destination. After setting up camp, we spent the next three hours just sitting next to one another, not talking, just soaking in the view, letting our minds wander, and quietly enjoying one another's company. The sun began to set and the sky turned bright orange and lavender, reminding me of a picture on a calendar. I looked over at Art and saw that a tear was trickling down his cheek. I began to smile and he said, "What, don't you think men are supposed to show emotion?" "No, that's not it," I said. "The last line on a list of traits of the perfect partner I made over a year ago was 'sunsets make him cry.'" At that moment, I knew the life plan that had become so comfortable was about to change and I had to remind myself, *Never say never*.

Needs Versus Short- and Long-Term Goals

A simple tool for uncomplicating issues and opportunities and continuing to move forward is to make a list—yes, on paper. Find a blank sheet of paper—and in this case, the only reason size would matter is as a reflection of your willingness to be optimistic. Begin with three columns down the page; across the top label the first column "Needs," the second "Short-Term Goals," and the third "Long-Term Goals or Dreams." The key to this exercise is to actually see what you're dealing with rather than letting it all just whirl around in your ever-so-creative imagination. It's important to be honest with yourself when it comes to listing your needs. Try not to confuse "needs" with "wants"; instead, use some of those "wants" as short-term goals. The other important thing to remember is not to be afraid to DREAM BIG. Your long-term goals may be a list of things to achieve or places to go or may involve a shift in mindset.

Your list should include challenges you need to overcome or things about yourself you would like to change or improve. At different times in my life my list of goals included items such as (1) lose 10 pounds, (2) go for a walk three times a week, (3) increase my typing speed to 120 words per minute, (4) spend two hours every weekday with my children, (5) register for a class on business management, (6) take a two-week vacation (actually, that would go in my "Dream" column), (7) take on more responsibilities on a particular job, and (8) collect past-due child support. The list goes on.

Take a few minutes and just start writing what freely comes to mind. Once you have a few items in each category, push yourself to go a little deeper. Really stretch yourself to actually write down what YOU want, not what you think others believe you should want. There is no guilt or shame in this list.

Needs	Short-Term Goals	Long-Term Goals or Dreams

Once you've made your lists, the next step is to prioritize each column. You will notice that by prioritizing you have created a shorthand form of a life plan. Don't get all nervous, as your plans can change; that's why you write the list in pencil.

— COMMON THREAD —

Visualize your goals as if you have already met them.

Put your list in a place that you can access often. The surest way to achieve your goals or dreams is to visualize them as if you have already met them. It is widely believed that if you impose a thought on your brain in a clear enough image, it registers as an experience rather than merely something you imagined. One of the many books that explore this concept is *Psycho Cybernetics* by Maxwell Maltz. A number of successful athletes and industry moguls will attest to the widely accepted practice of visualization. Tiger Woods's father taught him to see the picture of the ball going in the cup and urged him to "be in the picture."

In 1971, when I was mustering the courage to get a divorce from my first husband, I attended a Psycho Cybernetics class, and one of my classmates was a woman who was practicing every day in preparation for an upcoming golf tournament. When she returned to the group after winning the trophy, the instructor ask her to relay her experience. She said, "I had played that course a number of times, both for real and in my mind. When I imagined it, I could feel the sun on my back, the breeze on my face, and I could smell the newly mown grass. I tracked every shot in my mind and imagined every inch of every putt, each one going straight into the cup. I even imagined winning, jumping up and down, and being handed the trophy. When I stepped up to the tee to begin the tournament, it was as if I had actually played the course and my brain just went into 'been there done that' mode. I wasn't nervous at all!"

— COMMON THREAD —

Treasure your failures.

As you set your course to places unknown, you naturally make some assumptions, and those lead to acceptances—or they don't. You can choose to settle for what is familiar or you can choose to go after the possibility to fail. That sounds a little strange, but the reality is, if you're never failing, you're not trying anything new. Based on personal experience, you learn your most valuable lessons from failures. They are the stepping stones to success. But that doesn't mean failure isn't intimidating or painful. Some people will actually sabotage their success and in essence create their own failure. I believe it's not because they're not capable of success but rather they are afraid that if they succeed, people will continue to expect them to be successful in the future.

I saw this phenomenon play out several years ago with one of my sons, Justin. I was becoming more and more frustrated with his choices as a young adult because I knew he had so much potential. One day while trying to discuss the issue with him, I said, "I don't understand why you won't try this new job. We both know you're capable and it would give you a chance to excel and gain some valuable experience!" He lifted his eyes, looked straight at me, and in a solemn tone said, "You don't understand. If I succeed, everyone will know I can do it and expect me to just keep succeeding. It's easier to just keep failing. After all, I can meet everyone's expectations this way." How do you defend against that thought process?

First and foremost, a person must want to succeed. If you aren't ready, for whatever reason, it doesn't matter how many opportunities are laid at your feet or how much encouragement is expressed from those around you. However, once you have tasted success, albeit small, you usually want to repeat it. Know what stimulates and motivates you, and let that knowledge guide your plan in a direction that will achieve that winning feeling inside.

Most important, know that no matter how clear and well-intended your plan may be, some things are out of your control and you must be prepared to alter your path. Your life will have peaks and valleys, and your true colors will surface most in the valleys. Almost anyone can bask in the light of his or her accomplishments, but it's how you choose to handle the challenges, the seemingly hopeless periods, that will crystallize who you really are. I'd like to share a couple of personal examples that come to mind.

One Saturday morning in August 1988, I received a telephone call from Justin's father. There had been a terrible accident, and Justin's half-brother Scott, who lived with Justin's dad, had been killed. He was doing what he loved, riding his motorcycle, two days after his 24th birthday. He was riding down a local street and was going about 50 miles an hour when a woman in a van pulled directly out in front of him without looking. Scott couldn't stop and tried to lay the motorcycle down in an effort to avoid the van, but he hit the side of the vehicle going full speed. He died en route to the hospital. I was stunned. Scott had been a part of my life since he was nine, when I married his father.

When I heard the news of his death, the first question in my mind was "Why? How could this happen? Why now?" He was just figuring his life out after struggling with drugs and alcohol in his early 20s. The next week was a blur. Although I hadn't been on speaking terms with Scott's grandfather for quite some time, this situation brought us all together in what seemed to be neutral territory for the memorial service. I was seated at the front of the room with Scott's father, brothers, and grandfather and hadn't paid much attention to who had come in behind us to pay their respects. When I got up to give the eulogy, what I saw brought a smile to my face and a tear to my eye. The room was filled to capacity and flowed out into the halls. It was a true testament to Scott's ability to make friends everywhere he went no matter what was happening in his life, and confirmation that you do have an impact on everyone you meet.

Fast forward.

About a year later I was struggling with bills left from my divorce, including loans I should never have agreed to co-sign. I had filed bankruptcy and my home was going through foreclosure. I knew I had to move to a smaller place and needed cash, so I decided to sell as many of my belongings as I could. I put an ad in the newspaper, and one Saturday morning a gentle-natured middle-aged woman showed up with a friend and a truck. She asked if she could walk through my house and take a look at what I was selling. After wandering around for a few moments, she said she would buy it all. I gratefully agreed, and she and her friend proceeded to load it all into the back of their truck. When they had finished, she took out her checkbook and wrote me a check for $200. At the time I felt as though my worldly belongings were worth a lot more, but I was in a bind and most of the furniture was old. The next day I went to the bank to cash the check. That was when I learned that her account was closed and the address on the check wasn't valid. I was in the middle of filing bankruptcy, I was losing what I had hoped would be a stable home for my boys, and now someone had stolen all my furniture! This was definitely not one of the high points of my life and was certainly nothing I had ever planned for.

All of these situations challenged me to the core, but I had a choice to make. Did I let them keep me down, or did I examine the situations and move forward with resolve? I couldn't change them, and the positive lessons I learned would serve me well in the years to come.

You will never have total control of your life, so write your plan in pencil!

We can't preplan around destiny, and it's up to us to do the best we can with what we've been given. Here is a story about a young woman who did just that.

Meet Sara Reinertsen

Sara was born with her left leg much shorter than the right, and she was fitted with a prosthetic limb that was extremely cumbersome. She couldn't bend the leg, so when she ran she swung it out and did a modified hop-skip motion. Still, she loved sports and playing outside, and her mom had signed her up for soccer by the time she was five.

She was the older of two children and was not coddled as a child. When the family went camping, Sara carried her own backpack and took her turn fetching water. She played tennis and learned to ski. Her mother said that she and her husband wanted her to have the same experiences as other children and thought it would build character in her.

At the age of six, Sara's soccer coach told her she just didn't fit in and directed her to go kick the ball against a wall by herself while her teammates ran screaming up and down a grassy field. When she was seven, her parents made the difficult decision to have her left leg amputated so that she could be fitted with an advanced prosthetic. By the time she was 12, she set the world record for female above-the-knee amputees in the 100-meter run. She now holds the world record in the 100-meter, 200-meter, 400-meter, half-marathon, and marathon races. Sara was inspired by another amputee named Paddy Rossbach, an Englishwoman who herself had run marathons and organized an athletic program for the disabled. She was married, was physically fit, and had a good job, and those elements of her life also inspired Sara.

— COMMON THREAD —

Never say never.

Sara has always pushed herself to work harder, practice more, and never give up, even when the odds are against her. Six months after learning to ride a bike, she won her amputee class at the International Triathlon Union World Championships in New Zealand.

In 2004, she qualified for and competed in the Ironman Triathlon World Championship in Hawaii. She was attempting to be the first above-the-knee amputee to finish the race. The race consists of a 2.4-mile swim, a 112-mile bike ride, and a 16.2-mile run. Sara missed one of the checkpoints by 15 minutes and was disqualified on the spot. Although she was heartbroken at the time, that didn't deter her; she went home and trained even harder, qualified for the Ironman again, and this time finished.

For many years, Sara's "day job" was as a sports reporter for NBC television in New York. A few years ago, an opportunity came up when a job opened with the Challenged Athletes Foundation in Del Mar, California. It was a cause she strongly believed in, and it would allow her to live in triathlon central. She now teaches other amputees how to run, bike, and swim and how to embrace their many opportunities in life.

To learn more about Sara, go to her website at *alwaystri.net*.

chapter five

If It's Predictable, It's Preventable...or Is It?

Life might not be the party we hoped for,
but while we're here we might as well dance.

UNKNOWN

There is a well-known public speaker named Gordon Graham who travels around the country offering training in the sensitivities of diversity issues and sexual harassment to the employees of various-sized companies. Early on in his speech, he gives examples of how people can think things through in a logical manner and make sensible choices. At the end of each example, he exclaims in an energetic voice, "If it's predictable, it's preventable!"

Predictable
Doing what you've always done means you will always be what you've always been.

Predictable
Settling for the bottom rung of the ladder means you will always be stepped over by those climbing to the top.

Predictable
Choosing to carry someone else's guilt means you will never have room for your own personal joy.

Predictable
Choosing not to become educated in whatever field you set as a goal means you should stand in front of a mirror and practice saying, "Would you like fries with that?"

It takes some life lessons before you are able to predict anything, but you begin gathering those lessons early on. I was only four years old when my mother gathered my little brothers and me in a corner and whispered fearfully and desperately, "Please don't cry. It makes your daddy very angry!" Although it wasn't a detailed explanation of what was going to happen if we cried, we knew what she meant and I learned not to cry—ever. We also learned that asking "Why?" resulted in far more pain than the answer was worth, so I stopped asking why, for far too long. It took many years for me to uncover the predictable effects of those learned behaviors, such as not showing emotion and not questioning people or situations. The good news is that once I exposed them, with the assistance of a qualified psychiatrist, I was able to adjust my decision-making processes and change the course of what could have been a very disappointing and potentially harmful life. If it's predicable, it's preventable.

At least most of the time. Unfortunately, even though you may recognize a person as not acting in your best interest and your experience tells you that a situation is predictable, your desire to help, change, or prevent something from happening may not be within your control. There is a clear difference between helping and enabling, and sometimes, even if a situation is predictable, the result may not always be preventable.

— COMMON THREAD —

Be careful not to love too much.

Sometimes when you help people it merely supplements their skills or temporarily relieves a portion of their burden. You can help too much, love too much, and cripple an already weak person by taking his or her burden on as your own. When you do this, it sends a clear message to people you're trying to help that you don't believe they are capable of handling a situation themselves, rather than giving them confidence in themselves and the knowledge that you believe they can take care of it on their own.

Drawing on my three-dimensional visual thought process, I began viewing life lessons as either a sack of feathers or a sack of rocks and imagined that we all carry our lessons in a wonderful multicolored carpet bag. The positive portions of the lessons are feathers and the negative portions are rocks. We can choose to find the positive lesson from any experience and discard the negative, adding only the feathers to our satchel, or we can choose to carry all the negative, counterproductive lessons of our experience and let them weigh us down. Being the eternal optimist, I firmly believe there is a positive lesson to be learned from every experience if we look for it, and I am an avid supporter of limiting the contents of our satchel to feathers! But just because something is predictable doesn't always mean it is within your control to make it preventable, especially when it involves other people.

— COMMON THREAD —

Being a parent isn't a popularity contest.

As a single working mom, my days were filled with chaos, busy schedules, a desire to overachieve both at home and at work, and an eternal hope that my children would manage without me. My bosses wanted more and more, and my children got to see me less and less. Work was absorbing up to 16 hours a day; my older son, Troy, was going to college; my younger son, Justin, was desperately lonely and, unbeknownst to me, had gotten involved with a group of young people who were equally lonely and equally bored, and we've all learned where that leads. After my divorce from Justin's dad and the tragic death of his brother Scott, Justin's father moved out of state. Justin was spiraling downhill emotionally but kept it all bottled up inside. I was occupied trying to survive and wasn't being as sensitive as I should have been. There was a huge chunk of our lives that just blended into an unidentifiable blur.

It was crystallized one evening when I decided to stop work early and come home. I arrived at about 8:00 p.m. (I usually didn't get home until 9:00 or 10:00 p.m.) and when I walked through the front door, Justin was curled up on the sofa with a pillow pulled close to his chest, in the dark, watching television. He jumped to his feet and said, "Hey! I'll need to see a picture I.D. You can't be my mom because she doesn't usually get home until ten o'clock!" You could have heard my heart break from a block away. For the next year or so I tried to cut back on my work schedule.

Justin and I had been invited to spend occasional weekends with my cousin Greg and his family in a small ranch community east of Salt Lake City. He had sons around Justin's age for Justin to do "guy" things with, and Justin seemed to enjoy the change in scenery. In the middle of one summer, my cousin called and invited Justin to go to southern Utah with him and his sons for about a week. After some nudging from me, he agreed to accompany them to their cabin. When I returned to an empty house I jumped back into my hectic schedule.

One evening a few days after Justin left, I received a telephone call from Greg. It began with, "Now don't get all upset, but Justin has had an accident. He fell off a cliff and has a compound fracture of his leg. It took us an hour to get him to the local hospital in the back of the pickup. They've set it, but there are some complications and they are airlifting him out to the hospital in St. George for surgery. Oh, and when you see him, his collarbone is broken too. He fell down a mountain and broke it the second day we were here."

Don't get all upset? Was he kidding? St. George was a five-hour drive from Salt Lake City. Just as I was ready to leave, his brother Troy came in. I told him what happened and he offered to go with me, but I told him he needed to stay so he didn't miss school and work. In hindsight, that was a big mistake. I should have acknowledged Troy's concern and allowed him to make his own decision. Instead I treated him like a small child, hurting his feelings, and he ultimately removed himself from a number of future family decisions. I left and drove as fast as I could, arriving in St. George in three and a half hours. I rushed into the hospital and found Justin's room, where he was being prepped for surgery. They had given him some pain medication and he was groggy, but he knew I was there. When he saw me come through the door, a tear trickled down the side of his dirt-streaked face. "Make it better," he murmured. "You're the mom, make it better."

The doctor had to hook weights to his heel during surgery and pull the fracture back into place before putting on a cast from his foot to his hip. The required recovery time for this type of injury was a blessing in disguise for both of us. Justin needed some help and I was the only one around to provide it, so I modified my work schedule accordingly and we were able to spend some short-lived quality time together. But being the strong-willed person he was (I think that's genetic), it didn't take long for him to figure out how to scoot and pull himself up and down the stairs from his room to the kitchen and TV, and I ramped back up to my usual crazy schedule.

Justin was spending a great deal of time alone and had become more and more involved with a group of kids that I didn't know and less and less interested in going to school. It didn't matter what I said or what type of incentives or punishments I doled out; nothing seemed to connect. I finally called his dad in California and told him I needed help. He showed up unexpectedly two weeks later, on Thanksgiving morning, and told Justin he wanted him to come live with him. Justin turned around, went to his room, and packed a few things, and they left. I was surprised, hurt, and silent.

A year later after a tearful plea from Justin, Troy and I drove over to pick him up. He was dressed in black from head to toe, his auburn hair was long and pulled back into a tight ponytail, his skin was ashen, and his cheeks were sunken from the weight he had lost. The light in his beautiful green eyes had gone out. The damage done in the time he was gone took many years to undo. Justin's father was an alcoholic, and he was usually drinking by noon. The school Justin was attending in Riverside, California, was in a rough neighborhood, surrounded by a locked fence with a razor-wire top, and police patrolled the halls. Students were buying, selling, and doing drugs on campus daily. He had immediately connected with a group of students who were equally unhappy and who shared his propensity for substance abuse, and the year he spent with his father was filled with drugs, fights with his dad, and lonely desperation.

In conversations with him years later, I asked Justin why he'd left without a fight when his dad came to the house that Thanksgiving. He said he thought I wanted him to leave and assumed I had already arranged it with his dad. When I asked him what I could have done differently before he left, he said he needed "edges"—boundaries. I'd been so concerned about making the short amount of time I spent with him positive time, I neglected to set limits. I thought I was being what he wanted. I was trying to be a flexible, "cool" mom; I was trying to be his friend. Communication is a valuable tool in life and parents don't need to be liked all the time—but they must be respected. Being a parent doesn't mean being your child's best friend; it means teaching your child valuable life lessons. Predictable? Maybe. Preventable? Not always.

— COMMON THREAD —

Pain encourages change.

After eleven years of being single, I married my best friend, Art, in June of 1995. I had aggressively pursued my career in commercial real estate, and in 1998 I was promoted to an area managing director with CB Richard Ellis and transferred to San Diego with my husband. The company I worked for was holding its annual global conference in Las Vegas, and I was just settling into the first of four nights in the Paris Hotel when the phone rang. It startled me out of a disoriented sleep and I glanced at the clock. It was 3:00 a.m. My husband was on the line and said in a firm, solemn voice, "Honey, Justin has been stabbed. He's been flown to the hospital and is in very serious condition. You need to leave as soon as you can and fly to Salt Lake City."

My heart was pounding as I tried to pack and find the first flight out of Las Vegas. The limited information I had been given was that the house Justin had been renting had been broken into and both he and his roommate had been stabbed. Justin had also been beaten with the butt of a gun, and he was in extremely critical condition. It was presumed by the police investigating the attack that the people who broke into their house were looking for money or drugs, or both.

This was one of the lingering dark ramifications of Justin being given his trust money from his grandmother when he turned 21. He always loved being the helper, the giver, the one others could depend on. The fund was his ticket to becoming the king of giving and his tool for becoming the ultimate helper. Unfortunately, the circle of people he had surrounded himself with found countless ways to spend it on drugs, alcohol, and parties. At one time he had eight people living with him in a two-bedroom apartment. When the money ran out, he just kept trying to be that "go-to guy," but the people he thought were friends were gone as quickly as the money was.

When I finally made it to the hospital, I found Justin lying in the bed with tubes and wires connected to him. Over 50 metal staples punctured his head to reattach his scalp where he was hit with the gun. When he opened his bloodstained mouth to speak, a strange, squeaky voice came out. He said, "You're the mom, make it better." Tears ran down both our cheeks as I held his hand and tried to comfort him without being able to scoop him up in my arms. He had a large bandage on the right side of his upper back, and I quickly learned that he still hadn't been taken into surgery. They wouldn't give him any pain medication, because they wanted him to remain alert so he could communicate with the nursing staff.

The doctor explained the reason for Justin's high-pitched voice: the knife blade had entered his upper back on an angle and had cut through his larynx. The nurses estimated the surgery would take about two hours, but four hours later the doctor finally appeared in the waiting room. He said there had been more damage than originally anticipated and the blade had also nicked the jugular artery, but he had made all the repairs successfully. I was relieved to see Justin back in his room, even though he was in a great deal of pain and was unable to communicate because of the tube down his throat. For the next five days I sat by his bed, and when he slept I wandered the halls of the hospital. No shower, no changing clothes. That is, when I wasn't rushing a few miles away to another hospital.

As we all know, life has a strange way of testing our limits. At the time Justin was admitted to the hospital I learned that his brother Troy's wife, Sasha, was in another hospital not far away. She was pregnant with twins and had been admitted a few days earlier with severe edema. Troy was serving in the military and was in training in Texas. The next day, I called her hospital to see how she was doing and found out that late the night before, her water broke and they had to perform an emergency C-section. The twins were born six weeks premature. I spent four out of five days in Salt Lake, commuting between the ICU of one hospital and the maternity ward and neonatal ICU of another. Talk about an emotional roller-coaster ride.

I had a lot of time to search the dark places in my mind while I was sitting beside Justin's hospital bed and haunting the halls of the hospital, questioning my actions, my decisions, and my intentions. *If it's predictable, it's preventable.* What could I have done differently? How could I have changed the path Justin chose to travel? That's where the whole philosophy of the human's gift of free agency comes in. We all have the opportunity to make our own decisions, our own choices, for our own reasons. People don't change until they reach their own personal inflection point—and that's usually a point where something very painful happens to encourage that change. It doesn't matter how much we love our children and how clearly we can see that they are making choices that will not be in their best interest; we can't control them indefinitely.

What did I learn from this life-changing experience? Family is more important than any occupation or career goal; time seems to stand still when a loved one may not see tomorrow; you can't force an adult to do something against his or her will; you must plant positive seeds when a child is very young. And I learned that being available with unconditional love is a wonderful gift for anyone.

What did Justin learn? He's been given a second chance at life, and he has no intention of wasting it. If someone were to ask him what September 5, 2002, means to him, he would answer, "It's the day I almost died and the day I was reborn."

Sometimes no matter how hard you try to help and how clear your logic seems to be, other people have their own criteria for making changes in their lives, and sometimes life itself makes changes you could have never imagined. It's been observed that people don't change until their pain is great enough, and sometimes you make changes based on other people's pain. We are creatures of comfort and usually need to be prodded to do something that is difficult or new, even when it's in our own best interest or the best interest of a loved one. Fortunately, we are also easily bored, and for some of us, that boredom translates into the initiative for stepping outside our comfort zone and trying something different.

I've written the next profile as more of a timeline than a story. I've done this because this format emphasizes the extreme highs and lows and snags life can throw at you even though you are making good choices, doing the right things, have great mentors, and enjoy wonderful family relationships. Sometimes life tests your warp and weft beyond your capacity to comprehend.

Meet Laurie Black

Google "Laurie Black" and you will discover these highlights:

- San Diego Port Commissioner
- Advocate for mitigating homelessness among the mentally ill
- One of 10 Women of Dedication named by the Salvation Army
- Winner of the Alonzo Award by the Downtown San Diego Partnership
- Awarded the Pinnacle Award by the Athena/UCSD Connect program
- Selected for the TWIN Award for Women in Industry by the YWCA
- Twice named one of San Diego's 50 People to Watch
- Recipient of the Quality of Living Award for her visionary leadership from LEAD, a national leadership program dedicated to developing engaged civic and community leaders
- Chairwoman of numerous philanthropic events
- Noted public speaker
- Chief of Staff for Congresswoman Lynn Schenk

That's a pretty impressive list, isn't it? Now let's explore the path Laurie traveled to get these accolades.

1958: Laurie is the first child born to Natalye Shrager, 19, and Howard Black, 22. In 1960, Laurie's brother Jeffrey is born, followed by her baby brother Brian, born in 1962.

1968: In an effort to help Laurie overcome her shyness, Natalye encourages her to run for secretary of her elementary school student body. She helps Laurie make flyers that read, "KEEP ON TRACK, VOTE FOR LAURIE BLACK." It is her first experience with politics and winning.

1971: *Life Snag #1:* Laurie's paternal grandmother commits suicide.

1977–1980: Laurie attends San Diego State University and majors in Women's Studies. Her life blossoms!

1978: Laurie travels to Washington, D.C., for an internship with Women's Lobby Inc. She finds she loves politics. She interns with Congresswoman Lucy Killea and President Jimmy Carter.

1980: She meets Bob Lawrence at an election return rally in San Diego and falls in love at first sight.

1980: *Life Snag #2:* Laurie's brother Brian is diagnosed with mental illness and hospitalized several times.

1982, July 24: *Life Snag #3:* Brian attempts suicide.

1982, July 25: Laurie and Bob get married and Brian attends the wedding.

1982–1986: Laurie works on a number of notable California election campaigns: for Tom Bradley, Lynn

Schenk, Jerry Brown, and Lucy Killea. All the while, Brian is in and out of the hospital.

1986: Laurie and Bob's first son, Alex, is born.

1988: *Life Snag #4:* Laurie has an ectopic pregnancy and loses the baby.

1988: *Life Snag #5:* Brian jumps off the Coronado Bridge, survives, and spends eight months in the hospital. He is finally diagnosed with paranoid schizophrenia.

1989: Laurie and Bob's second son, Dustin, is born.

1991: *Life Snag #6:* Laurie loses one twin fetus. The other survives, and Seth is born in September.

1991: *Life Snag #7:* Laurie's grandmother is diagnosed with Alzheimer's disease at age 72.

1992: *Life Snag #8:* Bob's successful development business suffers in the recession. Laurie has to go back to work. She becomes chief of staff to Congresswoman Lynn Schenk. The kids are ages one, three, and five.

1993: Laurie's father-in-law, Larry Lawrence, becomes ambassador to Switzerland.

1993: *Life Snag #9:* Brian is shot seven times in a police-assisted suicide attempt when he intentionally put himself in a situation that forced the police to shoot. He survives.

1995: *Life Snag #10:* After an intense election, Congresswoman Schenk loses to Newt Gingrich. Laurie is out of a job.

1996: Ambassador Lawrence dies and is buried in Arlington Cemetery.

1996: Laurie and Bob's fourth child, Madeleine, is born.

1997: *Life Snag #11:* It is discovered that Ambassador Lawrence fabricated some of his credentials and accomplishments. His body is exhumed from Arlington Cemetery and moved to San Diego. This causes deep humiliation for the whole family. Laurie recalls, "You know those news clips where you see someone peeking out the front door into a sea of media? That was us! It was a nightmare!"

1998: Laurie decides to shake off the stigma of her father-in-law and applies for the position of president of the Downtown San Diego Partnership, a very visible, powerful position. When the Board asks why she is qualified for the job, she explains that if she can run a household with four children in four different schools and four different schedules, this job will be a snap. (It may not have been a snap, but Laurie led with grace and wisdom; among her accomplishments, she spearheaded the Clean and Safe campaign [*www.sdcleanandsafe.org*], which would change the face of downtown.)

2001: *Life Snag #12:* Laurie's mother is diagnosed with atypical carcinoid cancer and given one year to live.

2003: *Life Snag #13:* Natalye survives the year, but two years later is diagnosed with brain tumors. She makes it through brain surgery.

2006: *Life Snag #14:* Natalye needs to undergo liver metastatic surgery; the cancer is spreading. She delays surgery to be sure she gets to dance at her grandson's bar mitzvah. She dances, goes into surgery, and loses half her liver.

2006: Laurie is nominated to become San Diego Port commissioner. The approval process is long and controversial, but finally, in May 2007, she is unanimously appointed to the Port Commission.

2008: *Life Snag #15:* Four days after Laurie's 50th birthday, Brian is killed in a car crash.

2008, November: Laurie is reappointed to a four-year term on the Port Commission.

2009, March: *Life Snag #16:* Bob is diagnosed with stage IV systemic metastatic malignant melanoma and given four to seven months to live. Laurie reluctantly resigns as Port Commissioner to focus on Bob and her family. Bob undergoes painful, debilitating treatments in hope he will live long enough to attend his daughter's bat mitzvah in February 2010.

It's exhausting just to read about Laurie's life! When we met, she was completely consumed with living one day at a time, caring for her family, and keeping up with Bob's care. She can't allow herself to think about next month or next year, but she knows she can handle whatever snags her life's journey will bring. The only thing predictable about her future is that she will do whatever needs to be done with passion, commitment, and grace.

chapter six

Tenacity:
The Fuel for Growth

*Become so wrapped up in something
that you forget to be afraid.*

LADY BIRD JOHNSON

For many years of my adult life I moved from city to city, state to state, and even out of the country. This was not wanderlust but because of my husband Lou's job. Each home lasted about 18 months to two years, and then we were on to the next job and the next city. It seemed illogical to try and establish any sort of ladder-climbing career when I moved so often, so I decided to be the best possible secretary I could. I liked to refer to my job as "training bosses." My typing talent kept me employed throughout my marriage and divorce, even though the salary was never enough to completely cover all my expenses. That's where the Needs and Short- and Long-Term Goals list came in very handy. Sometimes my needs and short-term goals were in the same column: groceries, rent, prescriptions, day-care fees. "Long-term" meant a whole month away! The experience sharpened my already existing skills, including those of caregiver, responsible worker, positive thinker, and creative accountant.

So much had changed since those earlier days! I had now reached what I considered the top of a very short ladder (more like a step stool) in my job, and I decided to look for something new. One day I took a long lunch hour and went for a job interview as an executive assistant. Once the interviewer saw my résumé and discussed the duties of the job, he determined that I was overqualified and that I wouldn't be happy working for him. It has always amazed me how a total stranger can determine from a 15-minute discussion what would make you happy.

But it turned out that our discussion led him to refer me to a friend who had been looking for help.

I drove to the office of a commercial real-estate developer located in a restored vintage brownstone building. Although I didn't know anything about real estate, I viewed the position as any another executive secretary job, and I knew I could learn the jargon quickly. The two partners owned shopping centers and office buildings and were about to begin their largest project yet, a multiple-building office park with retail space on site. My job would be to work with the partner in charge of operations. The salary was less than I had hoped, but although I had imagined something with more excitement and maybe a little greater upward mobility (and thus a potentially higher paycheck), I knew I was limited to a position with a fairly low salary. I had no college education and I needed a challenging job, so it was an opportunity nonetheless. Everything happens for a reason.

I was trained by another secretary whose method was to tell me, "Well, it's baptism by fire around here, so figure it out!" In hindsight, that was the best thing that could have happened to me. The peaks and valleys of my life thus far had given me a very solid foundation built on tenacity or, as some would call it, pure stubbornness. I was determined to prove that I not only could handle the job, I could excel at it.

Sometimes the only one who needs to believe in you is you.

Within six months, the job was becoming familiar and I was learning more about what the other staff members were doing. The firm employed an in-house architect who also handled the construction coordination for all the tenant improvements for new businesses moving into the various projects. The company had their own in-house property manager who handled all the day-to-day operations and interactions with the tenants in the various buildings and shopping centers. One day the partners fired the architect. I approached my boss and said, "I think I can do that construction coordination job; it doesn't look that hard." He doubted that I could handle it, since I knew nothing about construction, and he still needed me as his secretary. I agreed to try it while I continued to perform my original duties, and he consented with the understanding that when I failed, he would hire someone else to do the job right. Never tell me I can't do something. All that does is encourage me. My parents actually used that quality to their benefit as I was growing up. Whenever they wanted a task completed, they merely told me they didn't think I could handle it and sure enough, I did it right away.

Within another six months, the property manager decided to move to Las Vegas and handle the projects in that market. Once again, I went to the partners and told them, "I think I can do that property management job. It doesn't look that hard." I agreed to continue to handle the other two jobs while I learned this one. Once again, they told me that they doubted I could do it. I told them I wanted to try and they consented, with the understanding that when I failed, they would hire someone else to do the job right.

Fortunately my people skills far outweighed my lack of knowledge about construction and property management, and the professionals around me were willing to help me grow. For the next five years I continued to hone my skills as a construction coordinator and property manager on eleven separate properties.

When I was approaching the point of spontaneous combustion, I received a telephone call from a national headhunter. She said she was looking for someone to fill a property management position with a national company, and everyone she called suggested me. The job required a person with a well-rounded background in commercial real estate including leasing, management, and some construction management knowledge. It sounded like the job was custom made for me!

After three interviews, I had the job. The pay was better, and I had only one tired high-rise office building to handle. It would almost be like taking a vacation! Needless to say, it was far from a vacation; I had to bring the neglected property back to its prime condition and reconcile a stressful number of vacancies and an income deficit of almost $300,000. It took me almost three years to accomplish all the goals set by our team, but soon the building was running like a well-oiled machine.

— COMMON THREAD —

Always look for new challenges.

Once I'd accomplished this, I was bored. Some of my friends advised me to just relax and enjoy the ride.

To try and make things more interesting, I volunteered to work on a committee made up of a number of professionals from other real-estate companies, all focused on organizing an upcoming event. After serving on the committee for almost a year, one of the other committee members asked me whether I had any interest in becoming the property manager for a large portfolio of properties for his company. It was a nice compliment, but I told him it would be a lateral move and I didn't want to make another move unless it was a promotion. That is when he suggested I become a full-time commercial real-estate broker.

I had never considered working at a commission-only job when I was raising children, but by now both boys had left home. I decided to take a risk and see whether I could turn the opportunity into a success. I had saved some money to carry me through until I earned my first commission. I benefited from my many years of multitasking as a single mom because I was able to manage numerous transactions in various stages of completion at any one time.

I've always believed that there is a perfect job requiring all the skills women have acquired throughout time over the past 2,000 years: strong people skills, attention to detail, nurturance, and the ability to build relationships, work long hours, and be a good negotiator and problem solver, along with a willingness to eat cold food without complaining. A commercial real-estate broker is that job.

The rewards are what you make them. You are the captain of your own fate. It's not unusual for a hard-working seasoned commercial real-estate broker to earn annual commissions in the high six figures, and many roll over into the millions. The challenge becomes the willingness to put in the time. Your first year you are invisible; your second year you may be acknowledged, but those around you who have already earned their stripes are still waiting to see whether you have staying power. By the end of your third year if you're not making at least $100,000, you need to consider another career path.

Match Your Job to Your Strengths

Have you ever taken the time to seriously consider what your personal strengths may be? We all have traits that serve us well, we all have tasks that come easily to us, and we all have things we like doing. Combine that with whatever education you've gained, and that can be translated into earning potential. Pretty soon you are looking at a possible career path or a confirmation that the path you're on is the right or wrong one.

When opportunity knocks, open the door.

After four years in the trenches as a broker with a growing clientele, I received a call from the man who had originally hired me as a broker in Salt Lake City, Utah. He had since been promoted and moved to San Diego, and he had an opening for a managing director. He said I would have to interview for the position along with a number of other candidates, but he thought I would do a great job if I made the cut.

The position would mean moving to San Diego and choosing to take a salary rather than working on commission. I had to do some serious soul searching, because my business was growing and I knew I still had a lot of earning potential. I discussed the pros and cons with my husband and we decided it wasn't just about the money; we could use a change.

I flew to San Diego, interviewed with all the managers (twice), and was ultimately offered the position. I received one sage word of advice from the hiring manager. He said, "Don't try to be like the rest of the managers, who are all men. We need your unique point of view and perspective, not just as a qualified manager but as a woman." My husband was extremely supportive of our new opportunity, and before we could say "Surf's up!" we were residents of sunny San Diego.

That was the beginning of a very steep, very fast learning curve. Joining the management team of an international company was just the tip of the iceberg. It was an entirely different demographic: different people, different rules, and unbelievable housing costs. As we quickly learned, San Diego was more of an old-school, good-old-boy network than Salt Lake City. The good news was that we didn't have to shovel sunshine!

I was so preoccupied with my new challenges and opportunities that I neglected to understand the barriers my husband was facing. He would spend his days looking through the paper and going out to meet with various business owners and managers, trying to figure out how he could reinvent himself. Although he had a degree in finance and had run a number of his own companies, going to work for someone else was fairly new to him. Having spent a number of years moving, I was accustomed to the art of relocating: leaving family, reestablishing your "nest," learning about the new city or town, looking for a job, and integrating into the community. What I failed to understand was that for someone who had spent his entire life within a 50-mile radius of his birthplace, this move was a very big deal for Art. However, his diligent networking finally led to a man with whom he became partners, and they created a unique niche company that has grown into a very lucrative and rewarding business.

My last year's salary plus bonus in the real-estate industry was just short of half a million dollars. Not bad for someone who started out with nothing more than mediocre typing skills! Tenacity is definitely the engine that pushes you forward when it seems as though nothing else is working, and it's a relentless tool when the mountain you have chosen to climb is made of boulders.

— COMMON THREAD —

Don't underestimate the power of tenacity.

There are women around the globe who are wonderful examples of positive energy and the blossoming power of tenacity. Suzy is one such woman.

Meet Suzy Spafford Lidstrom

As she sat in her white, wood-clad studio above the garage, sunshine streamed through the big windows. Suzy was surrounded by hundreds of her watercolor and oil paintings, and characters from Duckport covered the walls. She had fully realized her lifelong dream of creating something that brought joy to others.

Suzy was born in Waterville, Ohio, in 1945. By the time she was two, the family had moved to sunny San Diego, and she has lived there ever since. Suzy has fond memories of drawing and coloring, trying to be as proficient as her older sister. Little did she know that all those drawings and craft projects would someday inspire her to become a world-famous artist and cartoonist.

She loved studying the work of such cartoonists and illustrators as Walt Kelly, creator of "Pogo," Charles M. Schulz, of "Peanuts" fame, and Norman Rockwell, and she loved the early Disney animated films. Observing Suzy's love for art, her parents signed her up for oil painting lessons when she was 10 years old. She shared her work with classmates and was encouraged by her family, friends, and teachers to do more elaborate projects.

Since her natural tendency was to please others, she stretched and tested herself, and the newfound appreciation for her ability continued to build her confidence. "I was inspired by early success and I didn't suffer self-doubt, which can haunt and hobble even the most talented. I wasn't afraid. Inspiration was self-perpetuating," she recalls.

Watercolorist Milford Ellison was Suzy's art teacher at Point Loma High School in southern California. She describes him as one of her greatest mentors. "He was built like a cookie jar and had a booming voice!" she recalls with a big smile and a twinkle in her blue eyes. He constantly challenged her and encouraged her to paint in transparent watercolors, a very difficult medium. She took to it readily, and in the summer between high school and the start of college, Suzy began exhibiting her watercolors and other art, and selling to the public for the first time. As an art major at San Diego State University, Suzy experimented with various mediums, and her passion for art was fueled by her natural desire to be creative. She says, "What inspires me as a watercolorist is light, color, the sun's shadows, passageways, pathways, different surfaces, and shapes.

I love to paint outdoors; painting from life and not a photo is food for my brain and refills my reservoir of imagery."

At the age of 18, Suzy became a charter member of the San Diego Watercolor Society, at that time the youngest person ever invited to join. There was a time during her attendance at San Diego State University when she felt conflicted about the type of art she was creating. Although she was an accomplished watercolorist and was well schooled in the use of oils, she kept experimenting with cartoon characters. Creating the whimsical art made her happy, and it also had considerable commercial potential. She continued to be torn between the encouragement she received from her college friends to create more characters, the attempt at redirection by her professors, and her heart-felt love for watercolors. Her vision for the future was to show her watercolor paintings in an art gallery someday.

In 1967, at an art mart in La Jolla, Suzy was approached by a couple who admired her cartoon characters and presented her with the idea of doing a line of greeting cards. The following year she began her greeting card company, SUZY'S ZOO, with a selection of eight note-card designs, drawn in pastels. The SUZY'S ZOO menagerie has since grown to nearly 10,000 images. Whatever Suzy does, she does with passion and tenacity, and those traits were the fuel for her future success.

As for where she gets the inspiration for creating the characters, Suzy says it comes from believing they are real. She has created lives for each one, along with the town where they live, Duckport. She has imagined who their relatives are, what each character's likes and dislikes are, and all that goes with inventing a world where she would want to live. "My best work is done when I am creating a picture that tells a story," she says. "It's the kind of thing that children who enjoy drawing do very well, make up stories in their mind. It's extremely absorbing, and very exciting."

When she's not creating new characters or enjoying spending time with her husband and their daughters, Suzy stays busy in her local Rotary Club, and at one time or another she has served as a volunteer on numerous boards of organizations such as the San Diego Historical Society, Sharp HealthCare Foundation, Voices for Children, and Hall of Champions She also has been active with the Girl Scouts of America for many years.

When asked what inspires her now, Suzy replies, "Probably all that went into my life so far!" One of her greatest challenges was the recent sale of the majority of her company and trying to reinvent herself in its aftermath. Suzy will always spend time creating and imagining, but her future plans will include more travel and more painting in the traditional plein-aire style. Seeing through her eyes what nature has to offer is, as Suzy puts it, "Magical!"

chapter seven

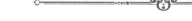

Lead with Clear Intention

If you can't be a good example,
then you'll just have to be a horrible warning.

CATHERINE AIRD

I love a good action movie. During a scene in the film *Sahara*, the main characters, played by Matthew McConaughey and Steve Zahn, are stranded in the middle of the desert. They come across a wrecked plane and, thanks to the imagination of Hollywood, they turn it into a tattered but sleek version of a desert schooner. A single sail made from one of the wings of the damaged plane catches the always-present desert wind, and a base made of some of the structural parts and wheels from the plane help carry it across the sand. Steve sits on the frame, trying to steer the contraption, while Matthew is suspended in a trapeze, much like sailors use on the open sea to equalize the weight of the boat. They are speeding across the sand when Steve yells up to Matthew, "Where are we headed?" With the wind rushing past his face, Matthew smiles and yells back, "I don't know, but we're making great time!"

Sometimes you may find yourself swept away in a surge, without a clear vision of where you're headed. Your pace is set by someone else: in your company, in your family, in your community, or even by unrealistic promises or commitments you've made. Once you are speeding along, it is very difficult to stop or even slow down without hurting yourself or disappointing others, not to mention all the people following your lead.

People following you? In life, you never know who is watching; who is committing to memory every move you

make, every mood you display, or the effects of your
efforts and actions. It could be a coworker, a friend, your
child, your neighbor, your partner, or a potential spouse.
No matter what you're doing or where you're doing it,
you are an example for someone.

— COMMON THREAD —

Everyone is a mentor to someone, even you.

It begins at infancy. Babies mimic those around them: their
parents, brothers, sisters, caregivers, and even strangers. As
a child, I'm sure you recall kids who were confident or
even pushy, and they were the ones everyone always
wanted to befriend. As a teen, peer groups are extremely
influential, and you are either a leader or a follower. As a
young adult you are deciding what to do with the rest of
your life, so you look to other adults for examples of what
success looks like as well as what failure resembles; mentors
on either path will be life-changing. Whether you recognize
it or not, you are a mentor to someone right now.

I would like to suggest that if you haven't already given
that concept some serious thought, it's time to start now.
It's time to accept the responsibility and do what you do
with clear intention.

Leadership doesn't have to be as apparent as you might
think. Leadership can take the shape of just asking

thought-provoking questions or looking at something differently. It can surface as taking the road less traveled just because it feels right to you, and finding others right behind you just because you took the risk or opened a door. Or it can be achieved through focus, vision, and crystal-clear intention.

When I began working in the commercial real-estate industry, only one percent of the brokers were women. Why in the world would I choose to do something so difficult? I didn't start out aimed at becoming a broker. I kept stretching, taking on more responsibility than I was trained for, and realizing that the more I was challenged, the more I enjoyed what I was doing. Being in the minority never seemed to be an issue for me. I was raised in a family of four children; I was the oldest and the only girl. Being expected to be responsible and getting along with "the boys" became second nature to me, so entering an industry that was dominated by men wasn't ever an issue, nor was it a conscious choice. What I realized was that I was naturally equipped with the tools necessary to become successful in this environment even though every move I made was being examined. My vast experience as a woman and a mom had prepared me well for the challenge at hand.

— COMMON THREAD —

Involving others shows respect and establishes rapport.

While working as a property manager and construction coordinator, I had just completed a large tenant improvement project in an office high-rise. The tenant's architect asked if we could meet for coffee and chat. She was extremely accomplished and knowledgeable about what needed to be done, but she always met with resistance when working with the various subcontractors. "I don't understand it," she said. "I was top in my class in college, and have designed and coordinated some very complex jobs, yet when I tell one of the workers to do something, they don't respond well. What do you do differently? Why do they always do what you want?"

I explained my observations to her: "When you interact with the subs you tell them what to do. When I work with them, I ask their opinion and lay out the plan that *we* have to accomplish. Your conversation is primarily about *you*, whereas my conversation is always about *us*. It's all about leading with respect."

Although I had no formal education in my field, I knew enough to respect the knowledge around me and I was never shy about asking one of the construction workers what he would do to solve the problem. Fortunately I was a fast learner, and as time went on I needed to ask fewer and fewer questions. I will always be grateful for the construction professionals who were patient and willing to teach me the ropes.

I found that clients trusted me, coworkers respected me, and I loved getting up in the morning to confront a new challenge. I believe the traits that kept my head above water throughout the 20 years I was moving from secretary all the way to managing director were my commitment and my passion. I was passionate about learning, about treating clients and coworkers with respect, and about being the best I could be and setting an example for other women. In real estate, the measuring stick of success is income. During a period toward the end of the first year in my brokerage career, I was getting nervous about reaching goals I had set for myself. I was talking with my youngest brother on the phone one evening, sharing my apprehension, when he gave me some very sage advice. He said, "Just do what you're good at and the money will follow." Wow, pretty profound for someone who was born a wanna-be hippie! But he was right. I needed to stop worrying about the money and just focus on getting the job done well. As it turned out, I was able to not only reach my goals but exceed them.

— COMMON THREAD —

Sex won't give you an edge.

As a broker, I met with a young woman who had interviewed with the manager of the real-estate firm where I worked. She was bright, attractive, confident, eager, and self-motivated—all traits that would typically serve a commercial real-estate broker well. However, during our discussion she made a comment that concerned me. She said, "I can't wait to work with all these men!"

Her first day on the job, she arrived at the office wearing a low-cut blouse and a tight, short skirt. It was the beginning of the end—designed failure.

The one piece of advice I've given every woman who ever wanted to enter the commercial real-estate field (or any other industry dominated by men) is to act as though the only thing the other brokers and your clients can see is your head. The minute you stop using your intellect and start using your sexuality, you've lost their respect and your edge. You may be invited to cocktails but when it comes time to work on an important transaction, you will not be considered. One of the greatest compliments I ever received was from a male client who said, "I love working with you because you are always such a professional and yet can still be a woman. Most women in this industry think they have to either act like one of the guys or sleep with you in order to get a deal done."

Fortunately times have changed, and there are many well-respected, responsible women in the commercial real-estate industry, most of whom depend on their intellect to succeed. As a managing director, I interviewed scores of young men and women who wanted to become brokers. Commercial real estate has been and probably always will be viewed as a very sexy, high-octane six- or seven-figure business. The candidates come from prestigious colleges and universities from around the country, and they all believe that they will be successful at whatever they try. Most are eager, self-motivated, and full of confidence.

When it came time to choose the one who would be most likely to succeed, however, I would always default to a couple of important traits: passion and the potential for leadership. You can teach almost anyone the rules of real estate but you can't teach passion, that fire in the belly. When times are good most brokers make money, but on the way up and on the way down it is the fire that separates the true success stories from the casual participants. My mantra was "Hire for the fire!"

The industry and our company were also embracing the value of working in teams, and if a broker didn't possess leadership skills, there was very little chance he or she would succeed on a team. Everyone needed to own his or her responsibility without being reminded of what to do. Catherine Aird, a prolific writer of mystery novels, once observed, "If you can't be a good example, then you'll just have to be a horrible warning."

The woman you will meet next epitomizes passion, commitment, and leadership, and serves as a very good example to all those who have settled for the status quo.

Meet Brigadier General Angelina Salinas, United States Marine Corps

On the drive to my interview appointment with General Salinas, I prepared myself to talk with a highly successful woman who had become a general in the United States Marines. I was wrong. I left the meeting clearly understanding that I had just spent valuable time with a highly successful United States Marine who just happened to be a woman.

As I sat in the waiting area with some of General Salinas's staff, we engaged in casual chitchat about Molly the resident bulldog, the recruits outside who were chanting cadence, and the weather. Suddenly the staff jumped to their feet and saluted smartly. "Good morning ma'am," the general's public affairs person said with respect in her voice. I turned to see a petite woman dressed in perfectly pressed fatigues with a star on each collar. She smiled genuinely and put out her hand. "Good morning! Thank you for coming!" I don't know why, but I expected someone more rigid, more serious, and more impersonal. Fortunately, those particular expectations were dashed within the first few moments. General Salinas was full of energy and possessed a welcome willingness to share her insights.

She began by confirming the purpose for my visit. "So you're writing a book. Tell me a little about it." I explained that it was nonfiction and would explore the common threads that connected women from all walks of life and how they turned challenges into success. I explained why

I thought she would be a perfect match for one of my chapters, and she smiled. "Well, I guess it's a good thing it's not fiction but if it was, I would ask to be portrayed as five foot six!"

Growing up, like most young children, Angelina thought that her lifestyle was the same as that of every other child. Her mother cleaned homes and did ironing for 10 cents a shirt, and her father was a mechanic. When she was eight years old, the family moved from south Texas to northern California to escape rampant discrimination. Although both her parents were American citizens, being Hispanic brought unsolicited challenges. They had hoped that the move would give their children a chance to flourish in an environment of equal opportunity.

Even in her earliest years in school, it was difficult for Angelina to carve out her own identity because the teachers were already familiar with her three older sisters. At home, when other children were out playing, Angelina was helping her mother iron shirts or working down the street cleaning motor homes. As she reflects back on those days, she smiles and says, "I thought my mom was the meanest person in the world! She always expected us to earn our way, and we always had to work if we wanted anything."

Now, in hindsight, she credits her mother for her strong work ethic along with her drive to always improve. She associated a good education with success, and when Angelina was invited to attend St. Vincent's all-girls high school, they couldn't turn the offer down. Angelina worked in a coffee shop to help pay for the private school and recalls that it wasn't easy, but it was an important turning point in her life. She embraced the opportunity to stretch her capabilities and grew to admire the nuns who were her instructors. At one point she even considered becoming a nun because they exhibited such commitment, self-sacrifice, and intelligence, and she wanted to be just like them.

She graduated from high school and with the help of work-study programs and scholarships, Angelina attended San Rafael College. She shakes her head as she recalls that her favorite subjects were parties and dating. She was failing most of her classes, and by the end of her sophomore year she was ready to drop out of school. Between her classes and working three jobs to pay for school, not to mention her active social calendar, Angelina was just tired of it all.

On April 30, 1974, she was walking into the post office to mail a letter when she came face to face with a handsome, articulate young United States Marine. He looked her in the eye and said, "Why aren't you a Marine?" She explained that she wasn't interested; she was just trying to mail a letter, but he wouldn't give up. He began to list the many benefits of becoming a Marine. She continued to defend her position of indifference, but after a long point-and-counterpoint debate he finally convinced Angelina that it was the best possible choice she could make.

When she came home and told her parents what she was about to do, her mother was on the verge of hysterics. Angelina's mother had always wanted her to become a lawyer, because lawyers always seemed to be successful.

Her father's response was, "Young women don't become Marines!" But she had already made up her mind. On May 4, Angelina stood in front of a U.S. flag, raised her right hand, and was sworn into the Marine Corps. On May 7, she was on her way to Paris Island on the East Coast to report for boot camp.

When Angelina returned from boot camp 12 weeks later, she was a renewed person. Her confidence and self-esteem had grown, and she says she finally felt as if she had found "it." "You know," she says with a smile on her face, "like in the movie *City Slickers* when Jack Palance said everyone had to find that one thing that made them happy and that *it* was different for everyone. He couldn't explain what *it* was, but you would know *it* when you found *it*. Well, I found *it*!"

When I asked what appealed to her about the Marines, she used words like *legacy, tradition, discipline, commitment, honor,* and *family.* Even though Angelina's parents wanted all of their children to become hard-working Americans, they were raised in a Hispanic family with strong traditions of its own. Family was very important to her, and when she talked about being a part of the Marine Corps, she said it was like being part of a very large family.

Angelina went back to college and graduated. She reversed her path from being at the bottom of her class to achieving the Dean's List, and her next goal was to become the first woman sergeant major.

One of her superior officers saw Angelina's potential and urged her to apply for officer's training school. At first she resisted, and even when she finally submitted her application she didn't really believe she would be selected. To her surprise, she was notified that she had been chosen for officer training within 30 days of submitting her paperwork.

Timing is everything, and this could not have been more true for Angelina. The year they accepted her into officer's training was the year the Marine Corps decided to integrate the men and women who were becoming officers. They would have equal training and there would be equal expectations. In October 1977, approximately 50 women began the 10-week training course, and 19 made it through the rigorous program. For the next six months, she was in school with the men, side by side with the four women and 35 men in her platoon.

One of the many advantages of being in the military is that you can set your sights on a goal and know exactly what you have to do to achieve it. As Angelina set about her journey to do the best she could, her path took her through legal services, recruiting, training female recruits, and earning her captain's bars. She had a natural gift for firm but compassionate leadership, and her well-honed work ethic and desire to stretch were put to the test. She constantly set her sights on the next rung on the ladder of responsibility, and she proactively kept a keen eye out for whatever opportunity would provide her with that challenge.

Once again, a superior officer who observed Angelina's personal and professional growth knew that in order to reach the next level, she would need some command time. Colonel Dale Town gave her that chance.

In the mid-1980s, a task force was formed to discuss opportunities for women in the military, and it was noted that the Marines needed a commander for a recruiting station. They needed to select someone who could essentially guarantee success in this post, and Angelina was once again given an opportunity to stretch her capabilities. She was selected for the command position and was sent to Charleston, West Virginia. She describes this experience as an excellent chance that would prove to catapult her career. She gives all the credit to the wonderful team of people already in place and expresses her gratitude for the opportunity to be part of the group. Along the way she earned her master's degree and was selected to hold the rank of lieutenant colonel.

A year later she was chosen to command the Fourth Battalion, which was comprised of approximately 80 drill instructors who would be responsible for the training of 2,800 female recruits per year. She describes the experience as "Powerful!" Angelina went back to school and earned the chance to become the first female to participate in the war pact and the first female commanding officer for the 10 western states, and her team set a record of achieving their recruiting goals for 39 consecutive months. This was unheard of, and she said she felt blessed to be part of such a strong, focused team.

When we took a moment to talk about how unique she was in her career arena and how important it is to be a positive role model, Angelina said that she felt fortunate to have been given so many opportunities to succeed. Although her schedule is very busy, she tries to take time to speak to young women's groups as often as possible and share her story. But she didn't always feel that way. For a number of years in the early stages of her journey, she didn't want to be seen as the "token female" and went out of her way to associate with organizations and groups that were made up of both men and women, never joining or speaking to groups that were exclusively female. She clearly recalls the day all that changed.

In 1994, Angelina accompanied her mother and sister on a trip to Texas to attend a relative's wedding. She and her sister were seated at a table in the corner and were discussing the appropriate time to leave and go see a movie. Although their mother was truly enjoying the opportunity to see relatives from years past, the two sisters didn't know many of the people in attendance and were not having nearly as much fun as their mother. As they whispered between themselves, the emcee of the event began announcing the names of relatives who had traveled a great distance to attend. The guests were standing and applauding, and Angelina's sister said, "Hey, they're talking about you!" As Angelina stood and walked toward the emcee, the people she passed had tears in their eyes, were reaching out to shake her hand, and were thanking her for representing them and defending their freedom. It was at that moment that she realized she wasn't just pursuing her career in the Marines for herself; she was representing all Americans, all Latinos, and specifically, all women. Angelina left the wedding with a new mission and a new vision.

Her performance and commitment earned her the rank of brigadier general and brought her to the Marine Corps Recruit Depot, Western Division, San Diego, California, where she would command the base, oversee the recruiters, and ultimately be responsible for the training of the recruits. She moved to the base with her mother and sister as roommates and set up her new home.

Since she is the first female Latino brigadier general in the U.S. Marine Corps, I couldn't resist asking Angelina the question on most women's minds: "How were you received on base?" She said that although nothing was ever said directly to her, she could feel a little apprehension from a few people when she arrived, but within a few weeks, she was accepted as "just another commanding general." Once again she smiled as she reflected, "It was the greatest compliment I could have ever been paid."

In August 2009, General Salinas accepted her new mission as director, Manpower Management Division, Quantico, Virginia. Her responsibilities include the administration, retention, distribution, appointment, evaluation, awarding, promotion, retirement, discharge, separation, and service records of commissioned officers, warrant officers, and enlisted personnel of the Marine Corps and Marine Corps Reserves.

Although her future plans include retirement from the military at some point, she is truly enjoying her journey and encourages young women around the country to consider joining the Marines if they are looking for a challenging and rewarding career. When I asked whether there was one thing she would like to see on her headstone when the time comes, she simply replied, "She was a good Marine."

chapter eight

Live Your Legacy

*Goodwill...is an immeasurable and
tremendous energy, the atomic energy of the spirit.*

Eleanor B. Stock

Legacy? Yikes! Legacy implies death, and most people don't even want to consider that eventuality, let alone actually plan for it.

To most it's a trite and fidgety suggestion, but have you ever tried to write your own obituary? The exercise is less about acknowledging your own mortality and more about pondering what is important to you, what you view as your value, and how you would like others to see you. I found that when faced with summarizing what I would like others to know about me, things that I *did* seemed inconsequential compared to who I really was, what I stood for, and the footprint I wanted to leave behind.

"Legacy" means something different to everyone. To some it's as simple as leaving money to their children or their favorite charity; to others it's making a personal contribution in their community in as many ways as possible. To all who choose to participate in the process, it is about sharing a passion and making a positive impact on your family and those around you. If you could touch the life of one person in a way that helped that person to feel better about him or herself and initiate positive change, chances are that person would be compelled to pass that gift on to others.

John Bunyan, a 17th-century writer and preacher, once said, "You have not lived until you can do something for someone who can never repay you."

— COMMON THREAD —

The simplest act will touch the lives of others.

As you pursue your journey through life, there will be countless opportunities to succeed. Some will involve just you; other opportunities will touch the lives of many. Some may be based purely on survival and some may be the result of intellectual visions made real. All will have been at least partially due to someone else's help or at a minimum, someone else's influence. It's important to understand that caring and helping others is its own form of legacy, even without being publicly recognized for your actions.

We've all known people who choose to bask in the limelight of success, neglecting to say "thank you" or, Heaven forbid, actually sharing the glory with those who participated in the effort. When a situation is considered viable because of the attention you will garner rather than because it's the right thing for you, your legacy will be forever negatively impacted, even if you're not consciously focused on creating one. When it becomes all about you instead of about the cause or the goal, people react accordingly, and you end up building thick tall walls around yourself blocking the light of goodness, rather than acting as a prism and letting the light shine through you.

Women historically have been viewed as the "behind the scenes" side of most equations, and it has been only in the last few decades that general perceptions began changing in a big way. That is not to say that there haven't always been strong, independent women throughout history who knew their destiny and pursued it at any cost. Those women were confident with who they were and understood the value and need for change agents; they were people who weren't afraid of being the pioneer, the first to stand up for a cause, the ones who knew the fight wouldn't end with them but who knew the cause was worthy.

Helen Keller once said, "I long to accomplish a great and noble task, but it is my chief duty to accomplish small tasks as if they were great and noble." Living your legacy will typically have a domino effect on others, either because you have provided them with an example of determination to follow or because you have helped them build the courage within themselves to make a difference on their own. Either way, it's a "we" action rather than an "I" action, and you can be assured something good will come of it.

Those who have voiced a commitment to a cause or have demonstrated a particular passion will tell you that it was ignited by something specific that happened in their lives. Some are dedicated to helping children, some to senior citizens, some to feeding the hungry, and others to saving animals around the world. Some have even taken on the lofty mission of saving the entire global environment. Thousands of organizations already exist that were established by caring people who surround themselves with other caring people, all dedicated to making a positive difference. There is still much that needs to be done.

In researching philanthropic givers and receivers, it's impossible to overlook the amazing work of the Bill & Melinda Gates Foundation. Their 2007 foundation assets were estimated to be $37.6 billion, making it the world's largest. Although the foundation is a combination of a number of funding sources, it is thought that Bill and Melinda will give away more than $100 billion in their lifetimes, and this entity is skillfully overseen by none other than Melinda Gates.

Melinda admittedly does not like the spotlight, but in her first profile, written by Patricia Sellers in the January 2008 issue of *Fortune* magazine, she noted that it was her older daughter who got her thinking about stepping out of her comfort zone. Melinda realized that if her daughter was going to have a voice in whatever she chose to do, Melinda would have to role-model that for her. Her natural tendencies for being well informed, her innate ability to understand people, and her invaluable talent for seeing the big picture have proven to keep her at the top of her game, no matter what project is her focus. Her positive influence on her husband Bill and others such as Warren Buffett and Bono continues to have an exponential effect, and it all began with a simple commitment to herself as a child. She determined that each day, she would set a specific goal. The goals varied, and would range from learning a new word to running a mile to being the valedictorian in an all-girls Catholic high school in Dallas, Texas.

At Ursuline High School, their motto was *Serviam* (Latin for "I will serve"). It's never too early to begin giving back. One of the many common threads that are woven through the fabric of successful people is their willingness and wisdom to surround themselves with other very bright and accomplished people. Melinda was no different. Another such successful woman is Patty Stonesifer, a living legacy in her own right.

Meet Patty Stonesifer

In 1997, Patty Stonesifer was ready to resign from 10 years of highly successful efforts with Microsoft. She had worked in a number of senior roles, and between her intellect and an ongoing technology industry boom, she had become a millionaire. She was ready to spend more time with her teenage children and move from a senior oversight position to one in which she could be personally involved.

As noted in a December 30, 2008, article in the *Financial Times* written by Andrew Jack, both Bill and Melinda Gates knew Patty was an incredible talent and did not want to lose her. Her personal wealth creation had given her an opportunity to practice the philanthropic principles instilled in her as a child. She had established a Seattle charity with her family, supporting women's and family issues, and she and the Gates shared the same beliefs in how people could, given the right tools and the right assets, be empowered.

Bill and Melinda invited Patty to visit a new philanthropic project in North Dakota to connect U.S. libraries to the internet. She instantly saw the importance of the project and as Melinda noted, "She could see where it was going and she would see ahead of Bill and me." Patty returned to Seattle and told them that if they could connect all the libraries across the country, she would sign up to lead the charge. It was the beginning of the Gates Learning Foundation.

Before 1997, Patty was a consultant to DreamWorks SKG and held a senior vice president position at Microsoft. As senior vice president of the Interactive Media Division, she was responsible for an $800 million business that created interactive entertainment, news, information, and service products. In addition, she managed Microsoft's investments in new online content and service products, including MSN. During her tenure at Microsoft, her division produced software titles including *Microsoft Encarta Encyclopedia*, Microsoft's Magic School Bus Series, and Microsoft Flight Simulator. In 1996, she negotiated a Microsoft and DreamWorks SKG joint venture, DreamWorks Interactive, which was subsequently acquired by Electronic Arts.

As the Gates continued to allocate many more billions to philanthropy, Patty helped to merge the entities with the William H. Gates Foundation. As their work evolved, it included medical research and global healthcare that led to the identification of the neglected space of investment in preventative technologies for diseases of the poor. They also realized the importance of using the spotlight that Bill and Melinda could bring to important issues by making them public advocates in a way that was very powerful.

In 2008, Patty was, in her words, ready to be "re-potted." She has transplanted her talents, passions, and foresight to another worthy institution, the Smithsonian, where she will continue to live her legacy.

— COMMON THREAD —

The true blessing of reaching out comes when you reach from within.

As we consciously choose our actions from day to day, I imagine it's much like weaving our personal life tapestry. Each day and experience is represented by a different textured or colored thread, and as time goes by we create our personal tapestry pattern. If you ask people what they would like their personal tapestry to look like when they are finished, I doubt that they would tell you they prefer that it was smooth and beige, surrounded by a wide empty border. Instead, most people want multiple colors and various textures, which are represented by bumpy nubs of conflict, silky strands of joy, and everything in between, with the pattern off the edge. We can't unravel the threads of our past, but we can make certain our future is filled with bright colors and interesting textures. Your pattern is your choice—weave with clear intentions.

I left the downtown San Diego Rotary meeting in 1998 with an address scribbled on a piece of paper. I wondered what to expect. The particular club I belonged to had a number of committees (60 at last count) that had been established for members, depending on what their personal propensities might be for serving the community. For those who are not familiar with the various national service organizations, the Rotary International organization was established in 1905 in Chicago by an attorney named Paul Harris. He was 37 years old at the time, and he gathered several businessmen together, at first rotating the meetings among the members' businesses (thus the name "Rotary") to network and help foster the ideal of service as a basis of worthy enterprise. Their motto, "He Profits Most Who Serves Best," was born in 1911 and in 1912 added the slogan "Service Above Self." One of the common threads that is woven throughout the lives of over a million members active around the world today is the adherence to the Rotary 4-Way Test, which came into being in 1955.

The Rotary 4-Way Test

Is it the TRUTH?
Is it FAIR to all concerned?
Will it build GOOD WILL and BETTER FRIENDSHIPS?
Will it be BENEFICIAL to all concerned?

When people unfamiliar with Rotary ask me what the weekly meetings are like, my response is immediate: "It's coming together with hundreds of my closest friends, many of whom I have yet to meet, but all of whom have a common goal of service above self, and they are all sincerely happy to see me. It just doesn't get any better than that!"

My personal service interest was helping children. I heard about the committee that helped provide support to a public alternative school downtown specifically operated for the benefit of homeless and at-risk teens. In hindsight, I believe I was drawn to it because during my 11 years as a single parent, Justin left home and was living on the street for a short time. I was still carrying a twinge of latent guilt (some burdens are more difficult to shed than others), and I thought that maybe I could help some other child in a small way. When I had spoken to the head teacher on the phone, she mentioned volunteer opportunities to mentor a student or help with various after-school activities, and that sounded like something I would enjoy doing.

As I drove closer to the address on the scrap of paper I noticed the streets were becoming more cluttered with litter, the buildings more run down, and gang tags were visible on a number of walls. The people on the streets looked like they might be drug users or prostitutes. When I finally found the address, it was on the corner in a row of run-down buildings covered in faded peeling orange paint, and with bars on the windows. As I parked the car and walked toward the door, I felt seriously concerned for my well-being, not to mention returning to the car with all its parts still attached. I entered through the battered door and found myself in the front of a cramped two-room space; one side was a crowded classroom filled with eagerly smiling junior high and high school students, and the other was a makeshift kitchen/storage/reception counter/waiting area. I was greeted with open arms and thus began my journey with Monarch School, originally known as the P.L.A.C.E., which stood for Progressive Learning Alternative Center for Education.

The head teacher asked me to remind her what I did for a living. When I told her I worked in the commercial real-estate industry, she said that at that time my experience would actually be an advantage. My first assignment turned out to be very different than what I had expected. The school had just been served with a 30-day notice to vacate because of massive redevelopment in the area, and I was given the task of finding a new school site. This worked out well for me, because I was currently employed as the managing director of the downtown region with CB Richard Ellis, the largest commercial real-estate company in the world, so it was, excuse my pun, right up my alley.

— COMMON THREAD —

Suck it up and drive on.

At the age of 17, while still in high school, my older son, Troy, decided to join a friend in the U.S. Army Reserve. At 19, he enlisted full time in the Army. Why?

"I feel lost, Mom; I don't think I'm getting much of an education." The military represented a sense of belonging. It fueled his personal need to represent a cause he believed in, and besides, his friend had joined the military after high school and was having a great time shooting cannons and camping out.

Before I knew it, Troy was assigned to Desert Storm. When I hugged and kissed him goodbye at the airport, in an instant, he was down the gateway and out of sight. I walked back to my car and realized I was shaking from head to toe. "Please, God, take good care of my baby," I prayed.

On one of our rare telephone conversations while he was overseas, Troy told me about the "Highway of Death." It was the desert path where tanks and trucks and bodies had been burned from fierce fighting two months prior, and his voice became solemn when he talked about some of the things he'd seen. His soul sounded sad when he said that he could have lived his whole life without having those images seared into his mind. When I asked how he was doing, he replied, "Like they say here, Mom, you just have to suck it up and drive on."

Since that frank and frightening conversation many years ago, I have applied that philosophy to many situations in life. When things are not what you expect, are out of your control, and there is nothing you can do about it, you just have to "*suck it up and drive on.*" Staying upset or frustrated doesn't help, and it doesn't change the outcome one bit. Each situation that relies on the "suck it up" philosophy is an opportunity for growth.

After an exhaustive search and the denial by more than 15 landlords, I identified a potential site for the new school. What I found during the search effort was that although preliminary discussions with multiple landlords would be fruitful, once I explained the nature of the school and the particular student population, the spaces I'd looked at just the day before would suddenly be unavailable. I finally met one particular property owner who didn't shy away from the idea of having a group of homeless students occupying his building, and once he came to the existing site and met some of the kids, he was even more interested in finalizing a deal.

When you say "homeless," the image that typically pops into most people's heads is a 50-something male standing on a corner or sleeping in a doorway. In 1988, that was the average age of a homeless person. Today, the average age is nine. Most homeless children don't make the conscious choice to live their lives this way. They became homeless by a series of choices made by their parents that propelled them into a frantic and terrifying cycle of poverty. All they can do is strive to survive, one day at a time.

These were the children who desperately needed the new school and the TLC provided by the staff and volunteers. These faces were the inspiration for a small army of community members to put on their "can do" hats and stay focused on the task at hand.

After a preliminary review of the modifications that would be necessary, it became apparent to a group of four volunteers that we would need to raise more than $1 million to remodel the existing building. That would be the impetus for us to establish a 501(c)(3) not-for-profit corporation so our prospective donors would be able to receive tax benefits along with the opportunity to make a difference in their community. We quickly formed a board of directors, and we all shared the same vision and were passionate about our ability to make the dream a reality.

We began fundraising right away, one dollar at a time. Our first large donation came from the wives of the San Diego Padres baseball team. Each year, they hold a fundraising event and donate the money to a worthy not-for-profit organization in the community. We would be the lucky recipients of a much needed check for $40,000.

We then organized a ground-breaking event and invited anyone we could think of who might be able to make a donation. I was acting as a host and talking with people about our vision, using an artist rendering as a visual aid, when an average-looking man walked over. He was somewhere in his early 40s, with curly hair, glasses, a short-sleeved white shirt, and khaki pants. The man was very quiet and shy and, well, looked sort of like a computer geek. He began to ask some pretty specific questions about the technology that would be integrated into the new facility and at one point, asked what it would cost to build a classroom. We had completed an overall cost estimate for the facility but hadn't broken it down room by room. Fortunately, I had some construction estimating experience and told him it would cost about $80,000. He casually reached into his back pocket and pulled out a checkbook, asked whom the check should be made out to, wrote out a check, and handed it to me. I thanked him without looking at the amount, then took a glance down to see that the check was written in the amount of, you guessed it, $80,000! I jumped up, let out a scream, and gave him a big hug. Only then did I realize it was Gary Jacobs of Qualcomm fame.

Within a year, we moved 48 students from a cockroach-infested slum to a newly remodeled state-of-the-art school thanks to more than 250 different subcontractors and donors. While construction was underway, the students at the crowded one-room school in the ghetto were being prepared for the move. The senior class had been talking (all five of them) and decided that this would be a great time to change the name of the school. They explained that every time they joined with other public schools for activities of one sort or another, they had to explain the name of their school and why they were different. The students suggested they hold a contest to find a new name that was more like the names of other schools. The winning submission was selected because, in one student's words, "it's just like we are." The name selected was Monarch because it exemplified the struggle each student endured, inching along like a caterpillar, and the optimistic possibility of rising into the sky like a butterfly.

By the end of the first year in the new school, the student population had exploded to over 150 students as a result of word of mouth on the street and students bringing their siblings. We realized that we needed to find another site and expand the campus to accommodate up to 250 students.

Why were we so focused and so passionate about this cause? Because the students who attend Monarch are there by choice, and they understand that the only way they will ever break the cycle of poverty is through education. Each morning they show up, even though some are coming from shelters, some from overcrowded hotel rooms shared with multiple families, and some are even sleeping in cars. Each of them understands that the people at Monarch, staff and volunteers alike, are there because they care and because they all have great expectations. On the wall in the reception center, a sign reads, "Restoring hope and unleashing dreams."

In an effort to stay connected to the cause, the board of directors began their monthly meetings with staff members or students from the school dropping by to introduce themselves, telling a little about what brought them to Monarch and a little about what they were doing prior. At one of the meetings the visitor was a teacher named Ms. Lora, and prior to earning her teaching credential she had spent the past 12 years as a police officer. She talked about the kids she would put in the back of her police car after arresting them for making some very bad choices. She would ask, "What are you doing? What were you thinking?" She said that by the time she arrived at her destination, two things always happened. The first was that every child, no matter the age, was in tears; the second was that they would all tell her, "Lady, you don't understand. Nobody cares!"

She decided to become a part of the solution by earning her teaching credential and began teaching at Monarch in 2003. She told a story about one of her junior high students who was chronically late with her assignments. The girl said she didn't like to do the work because it was difficult and she didn't think it mattered anyway. Ms. Lora calmly replied, "You have two choices. Either you can focus and complete your work or you can stand in front of a mirror and practice saying, 'Would you like fries with that?' because that's as good as it will ever get." From that point forward, any time students complained about the lessons or the work, their classmates piped up with "Would you like fries with that?!" Every staff member at the school shares Ms. Lora's passion for wanting to make a difference in the lives of homeless and at-risk children. Being given an opportunity to be a part of that legacy has truly been a blessing for me.

As I increased my involvement with Monarch, my husband couldn't help but be drawn in as well. During one of our evening discussions about what the future would hold for us, when he could foresee retiring, and what we wanted to do in our "golden years," he reminded me of a goal we both shared. We'd said many times that we'd always wanted to make enough money to give it away, but what did that really mean? Although we had been donors on many levels in the past, we thought it would be very rewarding to establish a foundation and be able to donate each year to a different organization based on the particular cause and its long-term effect.

It's not necessary to create a personal foundation to make a difference. Many people are learning that they can make a life-changing difference to thousands of women around the world through village banking or, as some know it, micro banking. A number of organizations have established a process and methodology to assist women in third-world countries start a business with a loan of as little as $100 to $200. The people who have participated in this effort can make a donation of as little as $25 each and by pooling those donations, thousands of women can start their own business and begin helping themselves. The money is repaid from the profits of the business and the businesses are simple, ranging from sewing to raising chickens and selling the eggs. Some women have established small markets, and others sell articles they make. All are hard-working, honest, and accountable, and many establish working pools where they are all responsible for one another's repayment of the loans. Failure is not an option. By helping with a cause such as this you are not only enhancing your personal legacy, you are helping others to create their own positive legacy for their children to follow.

No matter what your personal earning capacity or your age may be, you can begin living your legacy today, whether it is by volunteering to assist someone in need or providing an occasional meal for a family who would otherwise not be able to eat. You may be able to make a financial donation to an existing organization that can put the money to work for many individuals, and whether your name goes on a plaque someplace or you are the only one who knows what you have done, your personal legacy has begun and the world will be a better place because of it.

chapter nine

Good—Better—Best

*All that is necessary is to accept the impossible,
do without the indispensable, and bear the intolerable.*

KATHLEEN NORRIS

ecause I moved so often as a child, I cannot recall many of my teachers' names or even the name of the schools I attended. One thing I *can* remember is a slogan one of my teachers repeated often and even posted above her blackboard. (Yes, we had blackboards when I went to school.) It read, "Good Better Best. Never let it rest 'til the Good is Better and the Better is Best!" (I have since learned that the author of that quote is Saint Jerome, who is known to be the father of the Latin church and died in 420 A.D.)

This had a surprising impact on me as a child and stayed with me as an adult. I believe (although don't always practice this) that we owe it to ourselves to be at our very best physically, mentally, and spiritually at all times. Our overall well-being has a huge impact on everything we do. It affects our attitude, our relationships, and our ability to accept success as well as failure, and plays an important role in who we really are. As can happen with everything in life, this mindset can be taken to extremes: think of those pesky perfectionists who are never satisfied with how educated they are, how attractive they are, how thin they are, how many times they have been "first" in whatever they are trying to achieve, how much money they have, and how often they tell you about it—and the list goes on.

Trying to achieve wellness in a general sense is an important responsibility that we should all embrace. Once again, the "learn what we live" reality affects our efforts;

some are more fortunate than others. There are those who have lived among sterling examples of healthy living, ample exercise, mind-expanding educational opportunities, spirituality plump with faith, and a peer group who encouraged and celebrated personal growth, and then there are the rest of us.

In an age of overwhelming information about what is and is not good for us, you would think it would be easy to just choose the right thing. That would be too easy. Instead we tend to become numb to what we are supposed to be doing or reading or believing and do little, if anything, to work toward that illusive "best" in each of us. Many of us began our formative years with some sort of vision, some sort of dream about what we wanted to become or what our future would hold. That was when someone else was responsible for most of the daily "to do's." Then reality kicked in, and suddenly we lost our focus and became distracted by our daily existence.

In the omnipresent streaming video in my mind, I view the "best" as the fully illuminated prism I mentioned earlier. We each have been blessed with our personal prism, our personal three-dimensional opportunity to create unimaginable color combinations in our lives merely by putting ourselves in the right light. It can't be accomplished by staying in the shadows or by settling for the dim light of "good enough." It can't be achieved by closing our eyes to find the comfort of darkness, but must be encouraged by soaking up life's variegation like a sponge. Effort must be made to search out the bright light created by positive environments, positive relationships, optimum health, and selfless giving. That may sound like an insurmountable accomplishment, but it's actually the easiest path there is.

It's far simpler to nurture someone else's existing positive traits than to conjure up some negative methodology to tear that person apart. It takes far less effort to encourage good than to engineer evil, and even far fewer muscles are necessary to smile than to frown! People who have persistent positive attitudes are much more pleasant to be around than people who find fault in everyone and everything around them, and it has been shown that a positive attitude promotes good health and rapid healing. True natural leaders don't run in front of everyone hoping others will catch up but instead encourage those around them to grow, giving others the shoulders to stand on to achieve the next level of success. We've all heard the phrase "It's black and white to me," with black being the combination of all colors and white being the absence of color. What we've learned through the ages is that it's that vast "in between" that truly defines our lives—that zone filled with variations of every color known and unknown, every shade of joy, fear, hope, pain, anticipation, pride, and love we can experience that makes our lives enriched and so worthwhile.

Surround yourself with the best people— and the earlier the better.

Striving to do your best isn't anything revolutionary or new; it's an age-old mantra that is even integrated into something as elementary and familiar as the oath taken by Boy Scouts and Girl Scouts across the world. A part of the life lessons taught to young people in both these noble organizations is to work hard, help others, be charitable, be honest, be fair, and be true to oneself.

If you weren't a part of the scouting program at some time in your life growing up, you knew someone who was. I had brothers and was more comfortable interacting with them than with girls so the Cub Scouts looked like fun to me as a young child, but they weren't too excited about bringing a girl into their pack in those days. However, I could have benefited enormously by joining the Girl Scouts. A specific program that clearly demonstrates all the "be your best" traits is the annual Girl Scout Cookie sale. It teaches girls many of the lessons they will need when they grow up. They learn about entrepreneurship, marketing, sales, building confidence, setting and achieving goals, money management, teamwork, and so much more. It's far more than just a tradition or a fundraiser; it's a highly successful business adding up to $700 million in proceeds each year that helps fund the many programs offered through Scouting.

As an adult, I must admit I have been guilty of purchasing more than my share of Samoas, Tagalongs, and Thin Mints from neighbor children or co-workers armed with their daughter's sign-up sheets, but I always felt good about where the money was going. Who could have imagined in 1917 that a few pans of cookies baked by the Mistletoe Troop in Muskogee, Oklahoma, and sold as a service project would ever turn into the mega-business venture the cookie sales have become today? Today each troop and each council brainstorms and develops new ways, new sales opportunities, and new customer base lists and works to better its latest annual sales quotas.

The old standard for creating a successful business, "Find a need and fill it," was demonstrated in 2002 when a sales concept was introduced by the Girl Scouts San Diego Imperial County Council CEO, Jo Dee Jacob. For many years, San Diego has been a community highly populated by active or retired military from all branches of the service. Jo Dee herself is a retired captain in the U.S. Navy. Her personal knowledge of the military, her connections in the community, and the ongoing war effort were just some of the elements that led to the creation of "Operation Thin Mint" (OTM). "Everyone in San Diego either has a family member or a neighbor who serves in the military," says Jo Dee. "Everyone is touched by what is happening overseas. That is why Operation Thin Mint is so successful."

Now, when a cute little Brownie or Girl Scout offers to sell you cookies and you aren't an individual consumer, you can choose to purchase cookies for "Operation Thin Mint," and your order will be added to hundreds of thousands of others to be shipped overseas and delivered to service members all over the world. When you buy for the OTM program, you also have an opportunity to add a personal note of appreciation that will be included with your order and delivered with the cookies. The cookies are shipped and delivered at no charge and are truly appreciated by all the recipients. A soldier in the field reflected, "It's a sign that people back home are thinking about us and the cookies are definitely a big morale booster, a sweet reminder of home." If Operation Thin Mint isn't part of your area's efforts, be sure and ask your local Girl Scout Cookie entrepreneurs what their council's special project is.

The success of the Operation Thin Mint program speaks for itself—its millionth box of cookies was shipped in 2007, and the Scouts have no intention of resting on their laurels, or badges, as the case may be. Good, better, best...

The Girl Scouts of America was founded by Juliette Gordon Low on March 12, 1912, in Savannah, Georgia. Her story of overcoming obstacles and following her passion would change the lives of millions of young women across the globe. Here's a snippet about her simple beginnings.

Meet Juliette Gordon Low

Juliette Magill Kinzie Gordon was born on October 31, 1860, in Savannah, Georgia. She would soon be known as "Daisy" to those around her, and her love of the arts was apparent to all. She wrote poems, sketched, wrote and acted in plays, and became a skilled painter and sculptor. She loved animals and had a great sense of humor.

Daisy attended boarding school in her teens and later enrolled in a French finishing school in New York City. She loved to travel and spent a great deal of time exploring the United States and Europe.

As a young child she had lost hearing in one ear due to improper treatment of chronic ear infections. When she was married in 1886, she lost hearing in her other ear after a grain of good-luck rice thrown at the event lodged in her ear, puncturing her eardrum.

Daisy married a wealthy Englishman and moved to England. She continued her travels and divided her time between the British Isles and America.

Daisy spent several years searching for something useful to do with her life. Her search ended in 1911 when she met Sir Robert Baden-Powell, the founder of the Boy Scouts and Girl Guides, and became interested in the new youth movement. She poured her heart and soul into her passion, and less than a year later she returned to the United States. On March 12, 1912, Daisy held her first meeting of the American Girl Guides. They began with 18 young women, and her niece was the first member to register. The name of the organization was changed to Girl Scouts the following year.

From the original 18 girls, Girl Scouting has grown to 3.7 million members in 108 countries. It's the largest educational organization for girls in the world and remains one of the largest female volunteer organizations. According to the Girl Scouts website, 64 percent of today's female leaders in the United States were Girl Scouts and 82 percent of high-achieving alumnae believe Girl Scouts influenced their success.

Juliette Low has been honored for her efforts in numerous ways. She was commemorated on a postage stamp in 1948, and both a ship and a school were named after her. She was inducted into the National Women's Hall of Fame in 1979, and a new federal building in Savannah was named in her honor.

If you have ever asked yourself whether one person can make a difference, you need not look farther than Daisy.

chapter ten

Leave It Better
than You Found It

*Life is denied by lack of attention, whether it be to cleaning
windows or trying to write a masterpiece.*

NADIA BOULANGER

Any camper knows: if you pack it in, pack it out—and take something someone else has left behind! "Leave it better than you found it" doesn't apply to just camping. It applies to life.

If you take a moment to think about it, we're all given an opportunity to improve on every situation we experience, everywhere, every day. Whether it is something as global as leading a nation, joining our military, working in the health industry, protecting our communities, teaching our youth, being a caregiver, being a parent, or just smiling at a stranger you pass on the street, you can choose to leave it better than you found it. For those who say "It's not my problem" or "It's not my job," I feel great sorrow. If everyone felt that way, think about what our world, our community, our family would be like today. We all have a responsibility to make a positive difference in our world and in the lives of those around us, and it doesn't take an award-winning effort or a large sum of money to do so. This isn't a lecture; I am just making a conscientious observation.

At one of our recent Rotary meetings, the person who was asked to deliver the inspirational thought for the day recited a poem entitled "Your Dash." The author was Linda Ellis, and the message resonated with everyone.

I read of a man who stood to speak
at the funeral of a friend.
He referred to the dates on her tombstone
from the beginning—to the end.
He noted that first came her date of birth
and spoke the following date with tears.
But he said what mattered most
was the dash between those years.
For that dash represents all the time
that she spent alive on earth
and now only those who loved her
knew what that little line is worth.
For it matters not how much we own;
the cars...the house...the cash,
what matters is how we live and love
and how we spend our dash.
So think about this long and hard—
are there things you'd like to change?
For you never know how much time is left
that can still be rearranged.
If we could just slow down enough
to consider what's true and real,
and always try to understand
the way other people feel.
And be less quick to anger,
and show appreciation more.
And love the people in our lives
like we've never loved before.
If we treat each other with respect,
and more often wear a smile,

remembering that this special dash
might only last a little while.
So when your eulogy's being read
with your life's actions to rehash,
would you be proud of the things they say
about how you spent your dash?

I read this poem to my mother one evening as I sat beside her bed in the convalescent care center. She enjoyed it so much that I decided to read it to her friends and family at the celebration of life we held in her honor the following week.

Linda Ellis didn't always see writing and speaking as her career path. She was working for the top executives of a very large and successful corporation when she was touched by a letter written by the wife of an employee who was aware that she was dying. The words of that letter had a profound impact on her and she wrote "The Dash," which would eventually move millions of people. Based on a summary of her story on her website, *lindaellis.net*, Linda says, "I may not be able to change the world with these words, but I have certainly been able to influence a portion of it. The poem's words have convinced mothers to spend more time with their children, fathers to spend more time at home, and reunited long-lost loved ones. The words have changed attitudes, and changed the direction of lives."

Linda is no longer working for other people; she is busy following her passion, writing poetry, lyrics, and much more, most certainly leaving the world better than she found it.

— COMMON THREAD —

Appreciate the value of time— yours and that of those around you.

In today's fast-paced world, it's easy to get caught up in ambition and lose track of the little things that make such a big difference. Time becomes the enemy, and spending it doing anything that doesn't show immediate results is viewed as wasteful.

When I first went to work for CB Richard Ellis as a rookie commercial real-estate broker, I mentioned to the senior broker that I was planning to meet a friend for lunch. He said, "Is this lunch going to lead to business?" His question caught me off guard, and I quickly replied that I was just planning to enjoy her company. He said, "You'd better realize that you don't get paid until a deal gets done, so every minute you're not working on your business plan should be viewed as a lost revenue opportunity."

I took his advice and tried to be more aware of how valuable my time was, but I could never become so focused that I blocked out everything that didn't represent making money. That's probably the reason I never earned more than half a million dollars in any one year in an industry where your potential earning power is in the millions! Money doesn't always define success or define the benefit of an effort. It just happens to be the measuring tool for most of our commercial society today. It also doesn't determine whether a job should or should not be acknowledged or appreciated.

Consider this: How many times have you walked past someone who is doing a task or job you would not choose to do yourself, or is providing a service that is either a necessity or a convenience that you just take for granted? Take, for example, the people in Costco who are standing behind the little portable stations handing out samples of food or drinks. Or a security guard, a construction worker, or the nurse's aide who empties your ailing mother's bedpan. The list is practically endless. Have you ever done that job? Would you like to do it? Do you think it's easy? My answer to all three questions is "No!" Have you ever taken the opportunity to just say "Thanks for being here" or "Thank you for your hard work"? It sounds simple but believe me, it makes a difference. This simple act can mean a great deal to all sorts of people in all sorts of jobs.

In fact, researchers have found that gratitude is a key element of human well-being. Their findings show that grateful people are optimistic and energetic and deal better with stress and illness. Robert Emmons, Ph.D., a professor of psychology at the University of California, Davis, and psychology professor Michael McCullough of the University of Miami have completed numerous studies that have shown, "These people had more joy, more energy...they were just flat out happier."

Let Me Count the Ways

There are a number of simple ways to keep your "happy gauge" pointing closer to full than empty. One great tool is to include five things you are grateful for in your daily journal. You do keep a journal, right? If you don't, you're missing a wonderful gift to yourself.

Another is to dip into your "joy jar" each morning and evening. One of my friends gave me a joy jar when I was going through one of the many valleys in life. It's a simple container; mine was a canning jar used for making jams and jellies. She had written all sorts of things to be grateful or happy about, things to find joy in, on little strips of colored paper. She stuffed them in the jar, covered it with a colorful lid, and wrote a thoughtful note letting me know she cared. You can make your own joy jar or make one for someone else. Just the exercise of writing all sorts of positive thoughts helps to remind you about all the people and things in your life you can be grateful for.

There are countless other ways to make a positive impact or leave the world better than you found it. Try something anyone can do, such as conserving our resources by turning off the water while you brush your teeth or recycling your newspapers and aluminum cans. Just cleaning up after yourself at the beach or park or keeping your car in good working condition can actually make a meaningful difference to our environment. Try it sometime, and you might be pleasantly surprised by the results. You don't have to turn "green" overnight or follow in the footsteps of Mother Teresa or Al Gore. Just take some responsibility for your actions and use a little common sense.

The concept of leaving it better than you found it applies to both physical and emotional situations. Think of it as an opportunity to improve your environment without having to recycle your toilet paper. Okay, that may have been a little too graphic an example, but you get the idea. Great tools for this endeavor include being prepared to say avant-garde things like "May I help you with that?" or "Don't worry, I'll get it" or "I'm here if you need me" or simply "Thank you." You may be thinking to yourself, "That's just too easy," but everything good doesn't have to be difficult. You can try taking on challenges such as volunteering in your community or participating in a worthy fundraiser, or just helping a loved one through a tough streak of illness or unemployment. Send a card to a friend or neighbor just because you were thinking of the person, or read to an elementary school class or a bedridden senior. How about cutting the front hedge in your yard all the way across the top, rather than just the half that is on your property? (Don't laugh, because I've had neighbors who have trimmed only half the hedge!) There are countless ways to participate in making our world a better place. The key is to be a *participant* rather than a spectator.

If you think that leaving it better than you found it has to mean joining some global humanitarian or environmental movement, I would beg to differ. Every great crusade began with one committed, passionate person. Start your own personal effort to leave it better than you found it by integrating a few of these simple ideas into each day—you really can make a difference.

- Smile, often.
- Say "thank you," daily.
- Be kind.
- Be authentic.
- Help others.
- Don't waste our natural resources.
- Strive to achieve your intellectual potential.
- Be creative.
- Take a risk.
- Don't give up.
- Put in an honest day's work.
- Don't be afraid to love.
- Avoid gluttony.
- Respect yourself: body, mind, and spirit.
- Practice and teach tolerance.
- Learn from your mistakes.
- Pass along your good fortune.
- Leave judging others to a power greater than yourself.
- Embrace each day through the eyes of a child.
- Don't be afraid to think BIG.
- Never say never!
- Remember your Common Threads!

My Common Threads

A Collection of Worksheets

Personal Accounting

It is a good idea, every six months or so, to take a personal inventory of yourself. Sit in a quiet place, ask yourself these questions, and be brutally honest with your answers. You will be surprised at what you will learn about yourself.

What makes you proud? _____

_____

_____

What brings you joy?_____

_____

_____

What makes you smile? _____

_____

_____

Are you the best you can be, or is there room for improvement?

_____

_____

_____

Are you honest with yourself? _____

_____

_____

_____

Are you authentic around others? _____

_____

_____

_____

Can you help others learn the value of self-respect?

_____

_____

_____

Do I like what I see in myself?
If not, what steps can I take to make a change for the better?

_____

_____

_____

_____

Needs Versus Short- and Long-Term Goals

Take a few minutes and just start writing what freely comes to mind. Once you have a few items in each category, push yourself to go a little deeper. Really stretch yourself to actually write down what YOU want, not what you think others believe you should want. There is no guilt or shame in this list.

Needs	Short-Term Goals	Long-Term Goals or Dreams

Once you've made your lists, the next step is to prioritize each column. You will notice that by prioritizing you have created a shorthand form of a life plan. Don't get all nervous, as your plans can change; that's why you write the list in pencil.

Match Your Job to Your Strengths

Make a list of your personal strengths, tasks that come easily to you, and what you like doing. Add to that your educational accomplishments, and your best job may become very obvious.

My Personal Strengths

_____

_____

_____

Tasks that Are Easy for Me

_____

_____

What I Like To Do

_____

_____

_____

Educational Accomplishments

_____

_____

Let Me Count the Ways

THINGS I AM GRATEFUL FOR

_____

_____

_____

_____

_____

_____

_____

_____

_____

_____

_____

_____

_____

_____

_____

_____

For My Joy Jar

THINGS I FIND JOY IN

_____

_____

_____

_____

_____

Living My Legacy

HOW CAN I GIVE BACK?

_____

_____

_____

_____

_____

_____

_____

Who Can I Count On?

_____
_____
_____
_____
_____
_____
_____

Who Is Counting On Me?

_____
_____
_____
_____
_____
_____
_____

Index

About the Author

Michelle Candland was born in Los Angeles California and was the older sister to three brothers. By the time she was three she had already learned the painful consequence of upsetting her alcoholic father, had witnessed her mother learning to please as a survival mechanism, and was well on her way to accepting abuse as a normal way of life.

Her parents divorced when she was six, and at the age of eight, Michelle's responsibilities included cleaning the house, getting dinner started, and tending her two younger brothers when her mother was at work. She smiles when she says, "I feel like I've been a mom all my life!" The negative lessons she learned prior to the age of six would guide her down numerous paths cluttered with missteps, poor decisions, and misguided loyalties but the positive ones would give her the strength to never give up, the belief in a power greater than herself, and the desire to make a difference in the world.

Michelle transformed her relationship inadequacies into an enviable marriage to her best friend, and her numerous short-term job experiences blossomed into a rewarding 20-year career in commercial real estate. Her community involvement with Rotary International has provided her with a robust pool of numerous opportunities to give back to the community and reap the blessings of service above self.

Michelle understands that she is not alone in her experiences and is passionate about sharing her life lessons with others. Visit her website at *www.michellecandland.com* to learn more about connecting with her, inviting her to speak to your organization and sharing your experiences.